WHERE

A BEGINNER'S GUIDE
TO ADVANCED SPIRITUALITY

Rabbi Dan Ehrenkrantz's marvelous book *Where are You?* is an affable and illuminating guide to the secrets of the self.

—*Pir Zia Inayat Khan,*
president of the Inayati order of Sufism

An exquisitely wise book about what a human life is, and how best to live it. *Where Are You?* offers inspiration, insight and guidance, and left me a changed, and maybe even better, person.

—*Noah Efron,*
founding chair of the interdisciplinary program,
Science, Technology, and Society at Bar Ilan University

Where Are You? offers incredible clarity with well-organized insights and ideas. It draws us towards experience and the importance of the heart. This is a powerful and practical guide to a true and deeply spiritual life.

—*Jonathan Ellerby PhD,*
bestselling author of Return to the Sacred

With very little jargon, and in easy-to-read, flowing prose, Ehrenkrantz prods the reader with insights and questions to take the inner steps towards answering some of the big questions of existence. The book skillfully references teachings and examples from faith traditions, but is not overly beholden to any one, and so is equally accessible to all seekers/readers. This book enters a crowded field of books of teachings and guides to practice — this is among the best that I've read. Give yourself a gift, check it out, and sit with its teachings, letting them percolate into your life.

—*Dr. Jeremy Benstein, co-founder of the Heschel Center for*
Sustainability

WHERE ARE YOU?

A BEGINNER'S GUIDE
TO
ADVANCED SPIRITUALITY

DAN EHRENKRANTZ

Published in 2022 by

Spinoza Press

Copyright © 2022 Dan Ehrenkrantz

ISBN (paperback) 979-8-9858081-0-0
ISBN (hardback) 979-8-9858081-3-1
ISBN (ebook) 979-8-9858081-1-7
ISBN (audiobook): 979-8-9858081-2-4

Cover Design by Rupa Limbu
Interior Layout by designforwriters.com

To Joe and Eliav

CONTENTS

Introduction

You are not who you think you are.

That is because you can't discover who you are solely through thinking.

Thinking can be a helpful tool to discovering who you are, but if it is the only tool you use, you will create false beliefs. These false beliefs cause a great deal of suffering. This book is designed to help you see through these false beliefs and begin to explore other possibilities.

Intellectually, you may know that you have much to be thankful for but still find that you are often dissatisfied. Perhaps the guidance and refuge offered by a religion or a school of thought or system of beliefs hasn't lived up to your hopes and expectations. Maybe you pursue meaning and purpose, but they remain elusive.

For a long time, this was my experience. Then, some years ago, a shift started to occur. I began to recognize my false beliefs about who I was. With this recognition, an undercurrent of fear and dissatisfaction that had been with me for most of my life melted away. A more satisfying experience of life emerged.

I want to help you experience this shift.

Growing up, I had many experiences of feeling I was part of something larger than myself. I intuited that there was something I didn't yet understand about life and about myself, but I didn't know what it was.

As a child, I associated spirituality with piety. Someone who regularly went to a synagogue or church, prayed, or meditated was, in my mind, a spiritual person. I wasn't motivated to pray or meditate, so I didn't think of myself as spiritual.

In high school, I began to ask questions about life's meaning and became a spiritual seeker. Spiritual seeking, I have discovered, is an endless search for something that always remains out of reach. I remained a spiritual seeker for the next three decades.

Spiritual growth can be a lifelong endeavor. But ideally, spiritual seeking comes to an end.

I wouldn't give up my years of spiritual seeking. The impulse to seek is what led me to find. But this game of hide-and-seek also sent me down many unhelpful paths.

After high school, I became interested in religion. I continued my spiritual seeking and majored in religion as an undergraduate.

My undergraduate studies fueled a desire to learn more—which led me to become a rabbi. It took six years of study to become a rabbi. I served a congregation for fourteen years. And then, for more than a decade, I was the leader of a school for rabbinical studies. More recently, I have worked as a consultant for nonprofit organizations. Over the course of all these years, I moved through different understandings of spirituality.

During my time with the congregation, I stopped associating spirituality with the outward forms of prayer and meditation. Instead, I saw spirituality as the lived understanding that your life extends beyond yourself. This extended connection might show up as an attachment to family, nation, religion, or God. And many other possibilities as well. I understood all these connections to be forms of spirituality.

I still hold to parts of this view, but my understanding of spirituality has changed. My earlier view was that I was connecting to something beyond myself. I thought I understood what I meant by the words *myself* and *connecting*.

I didn't.

The next step in my evolving understanding of spirituality was the discovery of a deeper truth about this thing called "me." I have written this book to share this understanding with you. I hope my words will act as pointers to a happiness and joy that many find elusive.

This is not to say that life will become only happiness and joy. Anyone who tries to sell spirituality with that snake oil should be mistrusted. But there are possibilities for joy in life that shouldn't be missed—and I missed many of them.

There is no final destination that, once reached, entitles you to declare yourself spiritually enlightened and move on. On the other hand, there *is* a fundamental realization at the root of spirituality that has either occurred or hasn't. If you haven't had this realization, this book can help you find it. And if you have had this realization, I hope you will enjoy hearing from a fellow traveler.

To get the most from this book, don't take me at my word. Anything I share has value only if you take the time and effort to experience it for yourself. I claim no special authority and no secret knowledge.

If you are open to change, this book was written with you in mind. You may be an atheist, agnostic, stoic, pragmatist, philosopher, or scientist. Perhaps you are a Buddhist, Christian, Hindu, Muslim, or Jew. You may be spiritual but not religious, or religious but not spiritual. You can enter and exit this book with any and all backgrounds and beliefs. The keys to benefiting from this book are a willingness to explore and openness to change.

I have learned from teachers who claim the universal applicability of their message and illustrate their ideas with Christian, Buddhist, Sufi, or Hindu literature. At first, I found the references to these traditions to be an impediment. I was comfortable with material drawn from my own tradition. I questioned the notion of a universal spirituality. Was I being proselytized? Was I being asked to accept hidden assumptions?

Over time, I found the claim of universal applicability was justified. These teachers weren't attempting to proselytize, nor were they asking me to accept hidden assumptions. They were sharing stories and literature that had inspired and helped them. It took some time, but I learned to appreciate the material from other traditions without fear or resistance.

Although much has changed, we can still learn from the wisdom of the ancients. And deep meaning can be found in teachings from traditions other than our own. There is something powerful in seeing our personal experiences reflected in the words of those who have grappled with the same questions that preoccupy us. Across time and across cultures, we are united in the adventure of being human.

But while I draw from the wisdom of multiple traditions throughout this book, not all traditions are represented. This is due to my personal exposure and should not be seen as a comment on a particular tradition. I have immersed myself most deeply in Jewish sources, and this immersion comes through in the examples I share.

Jewish literature is vast. It contains many wonderful insights and many problematic passages. For example, the Bible has served as an inspiration for people seeking freedom. And it has also inspired enslavers.

Bible stories lend themselves to a variety of interpretations. Similarly, the U.S. Constitution can be interpreted to produce many different versions of America. The Constitution, and the Bible, aren't going away anytime soon. Offering new interpretations of the texts that lie at the foundation of our culture can be a powerful lever for change.

This is not a book for learning about Judaism or any other religion or culture. It does not encourage identification with a particular religion or school of thought. Nor does it discourage such identification. The insights within this book are compatible with any religion and with no religion.

Spirituality doesn't belong to any particular religion, nor does it belong to religion in general. Many books are designed for people who want to explore spirituality from within a particular religion or school of thought. This is not one of those books. This book explores a universal spirituality that is available to all.

I recognize that the sources I draw upon, including the Hebrew Bible, will be an impediment to some and helpful for others. If your prior experience with this literature has created resistance, I encourage you to persevere. Ultimately, I benefited from the religious literature used by other teachers. Perhaps you will have a similar experience. And even if your resistance remains in place, the essence of a teaching doesn't rely on the stories one uses to illustrate it. Love the Bible, hate the Bible, or anything in between—it doesn't matter.

If you are interested in challenging your current beliefs and discovering who you are, keep reading.

However, it's easy to *say* that you're interested in discovering who you are. Dedicating the energy necessary for this discovery is another matter. Understand that this will take some effort on your part.

The insights within this book are like musical notes on a page with no musician to play them. If this book has the power to transform, it will be because you are the artist who has given the words life.

Where Are You? A Beginner's Guide to Advanced Spirituality is divided into two parts. Part 1 is designed to take you on a journey to spiritual awakening. Part 2 explores life from within the awakened state.

PART 1

SPIRITUAL AWAKENING

Chapter 1

The Fundamental Question

*They heard the voice of God walking in the garden, like
a day-breeze.*
*Adam and Eve hid themselves from God among the
trees of the garden.*
*God called to Adam and said to him, "Where are you?
[Ayekah?]"*

—Genesis 3:8–9

THE VAST MAJORITY OF OUR thoughts contain an
unexamined premise. And we have strong defense
mechanisms devoted to making sure we don't examine
it. These mechanisms are so strong that you may find
yourself becoming defensive as you read this chapter.

Throughout our lives, we attend to our emotions and
thoughts in one way or another. We may repress them
or indulge them, but our thoughts and emotions are
usually at the center of our existence. "I want... I feel...
I think... I like... I don't like..."

Even when these exact words aren't said, they are
often assumed.

Although "I" is the subject around which most of our thoughts and emotions revolve, we remain a mystery to ourselves. Quizzes and surveys that hold out the promise of penetrating this mystery are internet clickbait.

Which Disney character, Harry Potter character, famous artist, etc., are you?

There are three types of leaders. Which type are you?

There are five body types—which is yours?

These quizzes and surveys take advantage of our desire to know more about this thing we call "I."

The fundamental question is, "What am I?"

> Seeing things as they are is the goal of spirituality.

This question, when asked correctly, can be a powerful gateway to seeing things as they are instead of as we imagine them to be.

Seeing things as they are is the goal of spirituality.

An even better version of this question is "WhoWhat-Where am I?" but it is difficult for the mind to absorb this question without some practice. For the moment, let's just ask, "What am I?"

What are you?

Before rushing to answer, notice your internal response to the question.

Do you take the question seriously? Do you want to provide a quick answer? Perhaps you didn't pause long enough to give the question close consideration.

We are fascinated with quizzes and surveys that claim to tell us *about* ourselves. Yet when we are asked the fundamental question, "What am I?" many of us want to move on as quickly as possible. We often prefer to assume we know the answer and therefore can jump to learning about this "I." What are its likes, moods, and motivations? How is my "I" different from, or similar to, other peoples' "I"?

But what if your understanding of "I" is not as clear as it could be? What if your understanding is fundamentally flawed, as mine was for the majority of my life?

Given the frequency with which "I" shows up in your life, wouldn't it be worthwhile to develop a crystal-clear understanding of what you mean by "I"?

Without this clarity, when you say "I think…" or "I feel…" what is going on? If what you mean by "I" isn't clear, then even if your thoughts and feelings seem obvious to you, you can't possibly understand what you are saying.

Trivilies are feeling happy today.

Without a clear understanding of what is meant by "trivilies" it is impossible to understand this sentence.

And without a clear understanding of "I," it is impossible to understand the sentence *"I am feeling happy today."*

For many years, I had thoughts, emotions, beliefs, and opinions without inquiring too deeply into the nature of this thing I identified as "me." I assumed I knew enough about what "I" was.

I didn't.

In retrospect, not examining what I meant by "I" led to many misunderstandings. And it caused a great deal of misery.

Instead of dismissing the question, allow yourself to approach it with a sense of curiosity. What, *exactly*, is this thing called "I"?

My body, my thoughts, and the way I experience emotions are all very different from what they were when I was three years old. But I was "me" at three. What is it that accounts for the consistency of "me" throughout my entire life?

In our first few years of life, we made rapid and remarkable transitions. We learned to recognize ourselves in a mirror. We sat, then crawled, then walked. We acquired language.

As we went through these transitions, we developed confidence that there is an entity known as "me" that provides an unbreakable connection to the earlier versions of ourselves. But if we are asked to locate this "me," we don't always know where to look.

In the Garden of Eden story, the search for this "me" begins after Adam and Eve eat the fruit of the forbidden tree.

God called to Adam and said to him, "Where are you?"

In the Bible, the very first question that God asks human beings is "*Ayekah?* Where are you?"

When God asks, "Where are you?" what, exactly, is God asking?

Is this a game of hide-and-seek, with God playing the role of seeker and giving up after being unable to locate the hiders?

If that were the case, we might expect Adam to respond, "I'm over here, under the fig tree!"

If we assume that, from the point of view of the narrator, God already knows where Adam and Eve are located, then the question isn't about "where." It's about "you." The question isn't intended to provide God with additional information. The question is intended to benefit Adam and Eve.

"Where are you?" is another version of the question, "What are you?"

According to the Hindu sage Ramana Maharshi (1879–1950) this question is so central that "When other thoughts arise, one should not pursue them, but should inquire: 'To whom do they arise?'"[1]

Before eating the fruit of the tree, Adam and Eve had a childlike consciousness. After eating, they became self-aware. Self-aware means that one part of yourself is aware of another part of yourself.

Self-awareness implies that there are (at least) two selves. This self-awareness is very different from Adam and Eve's childlike consciousness, when they were "naked and unashamed."[2] Before eating the fruit, there wasn't one part of self that could be aware of another part of self. There was only a single undivided self.

After eating the fruit, Adam and Eve's sense of "I" had changed. It was no longer a simple unity. Their sense of "I" had become a complex web that was capable of rebellion, deception, and hiding.

Try this brief experiment: Ask yourself, "Where am I?" and attempt to answer without reference to physical space.

For the sake of the experiment, don't interpret "where" as asking about where you are on your life's journey. Instead, ask, "Where is my 'me'?" Can I locate that which has always been and will always be "me"?

Where are *you?*

Before leaving this question, take a moment to feel the uncertainty the question raises. Watch how your mind responds to this uncertainty.

What did you notice?

When I try this experiment, my attention moves inward. And when I try to locate this "me," it's elusive.

My left hand has a clear location. And I know where my heart is, as I can often feel it beating inside my chest. But where is "me"?

If the word existed in English, the question might better be stated: "WhoWhatWhere are you?" Using only one of these words—who, what, or where—presupposes a certain type of answer. And the question is best asked without introducing presuppositions.

What is this thing called "me?" Is it an entity living inside me? A core person to whom all other aspects of my person must bow? Is it a process of cells interacting—neurons firing up other neurons to create a mental image I call "me"? Is it the sum total of all my thoughts, emotions, and experiences? Or something else entirely?

If I can't identify, clearly and without ambiguity, what this thing called me is, and I can't quite find this me when I look within myself, then who am I?

WhoWhatWhere are you?

Ayekah?

"I think... I feel... I want..."

What is this thing called "I" that supposedly has these thoughts, feelings, and desires?

When I think a thought, am I the thinker of the thought or the entity to which the thought occurs? Clearly both, but is either of these the same as the "me" who was there when I was three years old?

When I feel a feeling, did the feeling arise from my "I" or did it arise elsewhere, and is it my "I" that interprets the feeling?

When I want something, does my desire stem from the experiences I have had over the course of a lifetime? Or are these desires an expression of who I am irrespective of these experiences?

When I was younger, I asked myself questions like "Is there a God?" and "What is the meaning of life?" and "What is my purpose?" I got lost in these questions. They seemed interesting and captivating. In comparison, the question "What am I?" appeared mundane. I lived with myself twenty-four hours each day. If there was one thing I knew well, it was me.

Or so I thought.

The big questions I was asking were the wrong place to start. They served as a distraction. Before I could get to these questions, I had to learn WhoWhatWhere was doing the asking.

For most of my life, I made assumptions about "me" that, upon examination, proved false. Eventually, I managed to leave these deep-rooted assumptions behind. The result was like waking up from a dream.

I had been walking through my life, thinking a fuzzy notion of "I" was living it. Once I abandoned the misguided notion, the entity living my life turned out to be different from the one I had always thought was there.

It is tempting to dismiss this question, *ayekah?* as unworthy of attention. We can tell ourselves that the answer is obvious. Or we can tell ourselves that looking for an answer will lead to endless contemplation with no satisfying resolution.

For many years, I was unable to bring sustained focus to this question. I see now that my inability to focus was a defense mechanism. It was an unconscious strategy I used to avoid the discomfort of recognizing that I truly did not know who, or what, I was.

If you were able to sit with the question, approaching it with a deep sense of curiosity, what arose for you?

Many people say they failed to find their "me," and so they stopped looking. Stopping the inquiry because "I didn't find it" is just another strategy for avoiding discomfort.

Key Takeaways

- The fundamental question is "Who What Where am I?"
- If this question can't be answered clearly, we can't hope to understand our thoughts, feelings, and desires.
- The inability to engage with the fundamental question is a defense mechanism, an unconscious strategy for avoiding discomfort.

Chapter 2

The Fearful Defender

*They heard the voice of God walking in the garden, like
a day-breeze.*

*Adam and Eve hid themselves from God among the
trees of the garden.*

God called to Adam and said to him, "Where are you?"

*Adam said: "I heard your voice in the garden and I
was afraid."*

—Genesis 3:8–10

God had told Adam not to eat from the tree. The
serpent encouraged Eve to eat, and Eve encouraged Adam.

Adam and Eve were faced with a choice: Eat from the
tree or don't eat from the tree?

The act of deciding demonstrated that Adam and Eve
had gained a new type of consciousness. They could be
told no, and they could choose yes. With this new consciousness came a new sense of freedom.

If you never disobey, it's impossible to know whether
your obedience is freely chosen, the product of coercion,
or a lack of courage.

The only way Adam and Eve could experience their freedom was by making a choice that was contrary to God's stated command. By following their own will instead of the (supposed) divine will, they discovered freedom. Their freedom didn't come through a magical quality of the fruit. Rather, their freedom was created by their ability to choose and confirmed by their decision to eat.

> If you never disobey, it's impossible to know whether your obedience is freely chosen, the product of coercion, or a lack of courage.

Yet there is a contradiction here. Apparently, it was in the nature of Adam and Eve to assert their will against the divine will. They were created, by God, hardwired to rebel.

Rebellion is in our nature. But if it is in our nature, then it is not truly rebellion. Humans rebelling is like salmon swimming upstream to spawn. It is what we do.

When rebellion occurs, it demonstrates that we are conforming to our nature. Rebellion is just another form of obedience.

It is a paradox.

This interpretation of the story doesn't require a belief in God. In the story, Adam and Eve are created by God, and it is God who commands them not to eat. If you prefer, feel free to substitute that life brings us into existence, and as we mature, we are presented with the perception that we can choose to rebel or conform. But given that it is in our nature to rebel, rebellion is yet another way of conforming.

Most of us have experienced some version of this story. As children move from childhood to adulthood, they need to separate from their parents. This separation is often perceived as a rebellion, but it is healthy and necessary. It can also be difficult and painful.

Spirituality doesn't require any particular belief about God.[1] It requires an open mind and a willingness to examine your experience. If references to God are unhelpful for you, stories I cite that include God can, and should, be read allegorically.

We want to belong, and we want to be free.

These desires are a part of us, irrespective of our beliefs about God. The story illustrates how these desires can appear to conflict with one another.

To stay in their garden home, Adam and Eve needed to follow God's command not to eat from the tree.

To be free, Adam and Eve needed to disobey this same command.

As residents of the garden, Adam and Eve experienced a deep sense of belonging. Nature gave them whatever they needed, and they lived in harmony with the animals.

They belonged, but they didn't experience the fullness of freedom.

When they ate the fruit, they began their journey into freedom. Their sense of freedom grew, but they no longer felt as if they fully belonged.

When we break expectations, disobeying our parents or not following cultural norms, we sense we are expressing our freedom. But doing so comes at the price of breaking faith with family or society. Our feeling of freedom comes at the expense of our sense of belonging.

What stopped Adam and Eve from simultaneously experiencing their freedom and their belonging?

The emergence of ego.

I use the word *ego* to refer to the process of identity construction.[2]

As process, ego is constantly attempting to assert itself. This is demonstrated by the fact that humans will put virtually any content to work in the service of constructing identity.

For example, if you use a particular pen and begin to relate to that pen as "my pen" then the pen may become part of your identity. Losing this pen might be experienced as a loss far deeper than its financial value. Even if you were given a new, identical pen, the loss might not be restored until you had invested the new pen with your identity.

Ego is the process that can take a pen (content) and make it part of your identity.

We often conflate processes with their products. For example, a product of the process of oxidation is fire. Yet we tend to think of fire as a fixed entity rather than an ongoing process. "Ego," as it will be used throughout this book, is not a fixed part of your mind. It is an ongoing process. The product of ego is constructed identity.

Ego constructs identity through objects, relationships, professional and familial roles, and more. And ego constructs identity through lack as well as through abundance. "I am a poor person" is just as prone to feeding identity construction as "I am a rich person."

There is nothing wrong with constructing identity. Our constructed identities are an important and necessary part of life.

Ego is not an internal villain that must be destroyed. Ego is part of the maturation process.

When someone calls out your name, it is helpful to recognize they are trying to get your attention. Associating a name with ourselves is part of identity construction. Identity construction is necessary and inevitable. Ego has a meaningful and helpful role to play in our lives.

Identify means "to make the same as." You construct your identity by making something outside of you, the same as you. Ego is the trickster that accomplishes this impressive feat.

Imagine that circumstances caused you to be raised in a different country. At birth, you were given a different name. You were brought up by different parents, in a different religion, and exposed to different political views. You also chose a different professional path. Yet, beyond all these identity constructs, there is still something that is unmistakably you.

Whatever you have "made the same as me," the contents of your identity aren't *actually* the same as you. They are constructs created by certain conditions. If these conditions were different, then your constructed identity would be different as well. In this sense, constructed identities aren't essentially "real."

When we forget that our identities are constructs, we become overly attached to them. We believe that if we lose a piece of our identity, we are losing an essential piece of ourselves. That is a trick ego plays on us.

It is possible to have an identity while being aware that identity is constructed and, therefore, on a deeper level, not who you truly are.

What You Do Is Not Who You Are

Take Yo-Yo Ma, for example. As a young man, Yo-Yo Ma was able to separate his profession from his identity. At age twenty-four, Ma was already one of the greatest cellists alive. However, he had long suffered from scoliosis and needed corrective surgery. The surgery was going to be complicated, and it carried the risk of nerve damage or even complete paralysis.

In recounting his experience before the surgery, Ma said:

I remember thinking, "Okay, if I never play the cello again, I'm fine."

In some ways it was freeing. Because you kind of say, "Okay, done that," and move on.[3]

Ma recognized that playing the cello was something he did. It wasn't who he was.

When we become overly attached to our constructed identities, we believe that these identities are who we truly are. And we will do almost anything to defend them. Through a trick of ego, losing any piece of our constructed identity becomes synonymous with losing a piece of ourselves.

But we aren't actually losing ourselves. We are losing a constructed, conditioned, imagined, contingent version of ourselves.

When we lose a constructed or imagined version of ourselves, we make room for the possibility of reimagining ourselves. Of possibly finding a self that is *not* imagined.

I don't mean, for example, that Yo-Yo Ma imagined he played the cello. I mean he may have imagined that his true identity was as a cellist.

"Cellist" was part of his constructed identity. If he were unable to ever play the cello again, something important would be lost, but it would have no effect on his true, unconstructed identity.

Upon realizing that "cellist" was something he did, not who he was, Ma experienced a sense of freedom.

Constructed identity is different from personality. Our personalities are the temperaments we are born with. Our temperament is a part of us, but it doesn't define us.

We all have personalities. And each one of us is different.

If two dogs from the same litter are raised in the same home, we expect them to have different personalities. The same is true for us.

Our personalities aren't created by our conditioning. Conditioning interacts with and influences our personalities. But our personalities exist independent of our conditioning. The idea that we are born tabula rasa, as blank slates, has been thoroughly debunked.

Our personalities are with us from birth. The work of identity construction begins as we learn to recognize ourselves as separate beings. This recognition begins to emerge at around four months of age when we first become aware of our bodies. Before that time, we possess a unity consciousness. We are incapable of perceiving any separation between ourselves and everything else in the world.

Unity and Separation, Freedom and Belonging

A newborn infant doesn't know it is a separate being with a separate body. Newborns don't have egos. Ego emerges gradually, as we come to recognize ourselves as separate beings and the unity consciousness we are born with gives way to separation consciousness.

Toddlers frequently say "No" and "I can do it myself." At this age, the process of identity construction is fully

No

underway. The ability to refuse someone else's sugges-
tion—"No!"—is an essential part of becoming your own
person. Adolescence marks another developmental stage
when it's easy to see the effort to establish a separate
identity. And for much of our adult lives, we are very busy
"becoming someone" and "making our mark on the world."

In the beginning of the story, Adam and Eve are
pictured as adults with the unity consciousness of babies.
Like babies, they don't realize they are naked. Then, in
a fruit-eating instant, they obtain adult separation consciousness, with fully constructed identities.

Ego teaches us to see the reality of individuality. It shows
us that we are separate beings with bodies. As such, ego
launches a journey into the exploration of freedom. Ego
allows us to explore freedom by asking: "What do *I* want?"

When you were first born, you didn't have a sense of "I"
capable of asking this question. As a newborn, you experienced hunger and wanted to eat. Or you experienced cold
and wanted to get warm. But these wants weren't preceded
by considering the question "What do I want?" The wants
arose even though you had not yet begun constructing
your identity.

Adam and Eve both asked themselves, "Do I want to
eat the fruit of the forbidden tree?"

Their ability to ask the question demonstrates that ego
had emerged.

A lion doesn't get to decide whether it would like to
be a vegetarian. From the perspective of ego, this makes a
lion less free than a person. Ego wants us to believe that

if the lion were truly free, it could make this choice. But this is a misunderstanding.

Are humans less free because, for example, we are unable to swim underwater like fish or fly like birds? From the perspective of ego, the answer is yes. This is one of the reasons humans have developed scuba equipment and airplanes.

However, from the perspective of the unity consciousness we inhabited before the emergence of ego, the answer is no. We are not less free because we are unable to swim underwater or fly. We may be less mobile, but we are not less free. The freedom of unity consciousness is not about what we can do, it is about who we are.

Our constructed identities are an important and necessary part of life. But if we never realize that our identities are constructed, we only experience egoic consciousness.

I lived within egoic consciousness for many years. I didn't know there was an alternative.

Living solely within egoic consciousness, I missed out on some of the most satisfying aspects of being human.

Egoic consciousness wants to burst through any perceived limits. It encourages us to learn to swim underwater and to fly. Egoic consciousness tells us not to be limited by our perceived nature. The ability to transcend our limits causes us to imagine our existence on earth is different from that of rivers, trees, and other creatures. Unlike the lion, we can choose to be vegetarian. We imagine ourselves to be both a part of nature and apart from nature.

The idea that we are in some sense unnatural, that we

exist apart from nature, creates a longing to belong. We yearn for the easy harmony with nature that Adam and Eve experienced in Eden.

But this is similar to what we saw with obedience and rebellion. It is in our nature to develop egoic consciousness, to learn to swim underwater, and to fly. These activities don't set us apart from nature. The disruption to our sense of belonging is yet another trick that ego plays on us.

Unity consciousness, which we inhabited before the emergence of ego, allows us to perceive the reality of belonging. From within unity consciousness, if we had the language to express it, "I" would mean the same thing as "we," which would refer to all of existence. Belonging is our birthright.

When we were born, unity consciousness didn't have to contend with the perception of separation. As egoic consciousness emerges, unity consciousness typically recedes. But unity consciousness is still a part of us. Egoic consciousness is layered on top of unity consciousness. Egoic consciousness may displace unity consciousness, but it doesn't destroy it.

As adults, we can recover unity consciousness. But to do so, egoic, separation consciousness needs to learn to play a different role.

Unity consciousness is able to allow egoic consciousness to play its limited role. But egoic consciousness typically blocks out the ability to perceive unity consciousness. In doing so, it prevents us from experiencing a deep sense of belonging. Yet we belong as beautifully, and as simply, as the trees, mountains, flowers, birds, rivers, and grasshoppers.

Stated differently, unity consciousness, which sees that all parts belong to the whole, can accept ego as part of unity. But an untamed egoic consciousness, which insists on separateness,

> We belong as beautifully, and as simply, as the trees, mountains, flowers, birds, rivers, and grasshoppers.

can't tolerate unity. Ego is offended by the notion that its separateness isn't complete, that, in a certain sense, its separateness is an illusion.

Separation is an elaborate construction built on top of the deeper reality of unity. In this sense, separation is not "as real" as unity. And this is threatening to ego.

Egoic consciousness insists that its rebellion is a true rebellion, not just another form of obedience. Egoic consciousness contends that it can transcend natural constraints. But in reality, what appears to be transcending natural constraints (e.g., swimming underwater and flying) is itself natural.

Ego tells us we are separate from nature—that we must battle with and conquer nature. But this isn't true. It's yet another illusion created by ego.

Humans are made up of the same basic substance as the rest of the world. Nature is our essence, not our enemy.

The Hebrew word for earth is *adamah* and the word for human being is *adam*.[4] The Latin words *humana* (human) and *humus* (earth) may be echoing the same idea. We have an unbreakable, intimate bond with the earth.

After Adam and Eve eat from the fruit of the tree, they are unable to simultaneously experience both their freedom and their belonging. Egoic consciousness blocked out their ability to dwell within unity consciousness. Adam and Eve leave Eden.

In reality, they never stopped belonging. And they were always free.

Fear and Dissatisfaction

On a very basic level, and when functioning well, ego exists to protect us. If there is no awareness of a separate "I," then there is no personal protective instinct.

Awareness of separation gives rise to vulnerability. As separate beings, we can be harmed and even destroyed. Ego protects us by keeping us aware of our vulnerability and constantly scanning the world for threats.

Ego is on guard against physical danger, such as an approaching predator. And because we rely on relationships for safety and companionship, ego pays close attention to emotional and social slights.

Fear is ego's constant companion.

Along with its protective function, ego urges us to make our mark on the world.

Ancient Jewish sources speak of the *yetzer ha'ra*, "the bad impulse." Although it is labeled "bad," this impulse is seen as a normal and potentially beneficial part of life.

> *Without the yetzer ha'ra, a person wouldn't build a*
> *house, find a spouse, and have children.*[5]

Ego is always dissatisfied with the status quo. This dissatisfaction provides the raw material that keeps the process of identity construction churning along. The drive to make the world conform to ego's notions of what is ideal leads to many positive outcomes.

On one level, we *should* understand ourselves as separate beings. And the desire to leave the world better than we found it is a valuable impulse. But no matter how much you may have achieved, ego never rests. Along with fear, dissatisfaction is ego's constant companion. Ego always wants more.

Fear and dissatisfaction prevent us from experiencing that the world is perfect, just as it is. "Perfect" here refers to an experience of the beholder. It is not a judgment on whether the world can be improved upon.

The experience of perfection is usually accompanied by a sense of gratitude and appreciation. Expansive gratitude and appreciation don't leave room for the experience of dissatisfaction.

When fear and dissatisfaction drop away, the imperfections of the world are seen within the context of the whole. Gratitude and appreciation don't require that we become blind to imperfections. Rather, the imperfections are seen and embraced.

The sense of "perfect" may also refer to the realization that things must be as they are. The future may bring changes. And the past may have contained other possibilities. But the present can only contain exactly what it contains. In this sense, the present moment is the perfect outcome of all that has come before and the perfect starting place for whatever the future may bring.

Even when appreciation and gratitude don't accompany the experience of perfection, there is still a deep sense of acceptance. Acceptance is about aligning ourselves with reality instead of fighting against it. Acceptance doesn't need to imply approval, resignation, or inaction. We may prefer that reality was different. But having unfulfilled preferences doesn't need to include dissatisfaction.

It's much easier for me to experience a sense of perfection when it's accompanied by gratitude and appreciation. I am frequently dissatisfied when the world doesn't conform to my preferences on what I consider to be matters of importance. This dissatisfaction is understandable. But resisting what is doesn't help satisfy my preferences. Ego's impulse to resist what is prevents me from experiencing that the present moment can only contain exactly what it contains.

Perfect doesn't mean that nothing should change. Perfect includes the ability to add to the world's beauty through human creativity and love.

In Hebrew, the word *shleymut* means "perfect, whole, and complete." One of my favorite Jewish folk sayings is "There is nothing so whole as a broken heart."[6] When tragedy strikes and our hearts break, we are part of the world's perfection. The depth of our loss is connected to the depth of our love.

Stagnation is not perfection. Unity consciousness holds the view that perfection can include possibilities for improvement. Egoic consciousness holds the view that if it can be improved upon, it's not perfect.

We are separate, but as we perceived when we were first born, we are also not separate.

The "bad impulse" is bad, not because it causes us to "build a house, find a spouse, and have children." It is bad because it sees only separation and individuality. It sows fear and dissatisfaction and blocks out our ability to perceive unity. When we stop perceiving unity, we are governed solely by the impulses of ego.

Fear and dissatisfaction can occasionally be useful. Perpetual fear and dissatisfaction are neurotic. And perpetual fear and dissatisfaction are the state we are typically in when we are governed by ego.

For much of my life, I would chase a goal, thinking its achievement would bring me satisfaction. When success appeared likely, the next goal would emerge. The new goal held the promise that its achievement would provide the satisfaction I sought.

Anything positive in my life was accompanied by a fear that it could be lost. And anything negative was perceived as a threat that needed to be managed or eliminated.

My fear of loss didn't help me. It only inhibited my enjoyment. And my efforts to manage and eliminate threats, while sometimes helpful, were often overzealous. I would focus on minor issues as if they had major importance. I could tell myself again and again that an unsatisfying personal interaction was not worth my attention. But it didn't matter. I would keep replaying the interaction in my mind.

The *yetzer ha'ra*, the bad impulse, is "bad" because it insists on being our ruler when its proper role is as a humble servant.

Most of us have worked hard to create identities that establish us as separate beings. At the age of two, we learned to stand up to authority figures and say no. As adolescents, we exerted a lot of effort forging our identities. And as adults, we have worked to "become somebody." All of this has taken tremendous effort.

When we were babies, our unity consciousness existed without the awareness of separation consciousness. As adults, our challenge is to incorporate separation consciousness within unity consciousness. But ego doesn't want to give up control.

To mature, we need to experience ourselves as individuals who are separate from the crowd. But ego believes that maturation is *only* about standing apart. It is threatened by the notion that maturation also means "standing together with."

The "I" that ego has spent so much effort to build will do whatever it can to fight off any threats to its existence.

God called to Adam and said to him, "Where are you?"
[Ayekah?]
Adam said: "I heard your voice in the garden and I
was afraid."⁷

Why is Adam afraid?

Being aware of ourselves as separate individuals makes us afraid. We are afraid that this "I" which we have worked so hard to create will disappear.

Adam was afraid that an encounter with God might destroy his precious "I." He believed his freedom and individuality could be taken away.

When Adam and Eve hear "the voice of God walking in the garden, like a day-breeze," they are afraid. They attempt to hide their newly acquired "I" from God, afraid that it will be overwhelmed and lost.

God notices that something has changed within Adam. God asks Adam, "Where are you?" *Ayekah?*

When Adam responds, "I was afraid," it is the newly discovered "I" to which Adam refers. This newly discovered "I" is the identity we construct to convince ourselves that we have "become someone."

The unconstructed self is not afraid of God. The constructed self is afraid of God.

Again, the message within the story doesn't require a belief in God. In this reading, God represents the unity consciousness of the unconstructed self. The insight offered is that separation consciousness is afraid of being overwhelmed by unity consciousness. The constructed "I" is afraid that in the face of a powerful encounter with unity consciousness, it will disappear.

As long as we're alive, this fear is unfounded. The constructed "I" may cease to dominate, but it won't disappear.

In our work of identity construction, new versions of ourselves replace the old ones. Each time this occurs, we experience resistance. Sometimes the resistance is subtle. And sometimes it's readily apparent.

Each version of our constructed self wants to remain. Even though our constructed self is confronted again and again with the inevitability of its own demise, it still resists. As our constructed identities fall away and are replaced with newer versions, we experience a miniature version of death.

And here's the bad news for our constructed "I." Eventually it *will* disappear.

At some point, we will die. And when we do, we will no longer be Americans or Russians, no longer prefer comedies or dramas. We will no longer exist in a form that can sustain our constructed "I" as we know it. The mental chatter of our minds will fade away.

Ernest Becker, author of the Pulitzer Prize-winning book, *The Denial of Death*, argued that "...the basic motivation for human behavior is our biological need to control our basic anxiety, to deny the terror of death."[8]

It is normal for human beings to fear death. But what, exactly, are we afraid of losing? From within the unity consciousness of the unconstructed self, we are part of the whole. The unconstructed self isn't afraid of death. The "terror of death" that Becker says is the motivation for human behavior, belongs to the constructed self.

Becker put it this way:

> *I would say it's the most important thing to know that beyond the absurdity of one's life, beyond the apparent injustice of things, beyond the human viewpoint, beyond what's happening to us, there is the fact of the tremendous creative energies of the cosmos…*[9]

The unconstructed self is our bridge to experiencing the "tremendous creative energies of the cosmos." The constructed self carries what Becker calls "the human viewpoint." It is the constructed self that is afraid of death.

The constructed self's fear of death is so overwhelming that many people devote the majority of their lives to staving it off.

Seen for what it is, the dance of ego is a tragicomedy. Ego emerges as we learn to explore freedom, and it exists to protect us. But to better play this protective role, ego fools us into believing that our constructed identity is who we are. Ego is now in the business of protecting ego.

In the movie *The Matrix*, machines construct a universe (the matrix) that keeps human beings trapped in an illusory reality. The hero of the movie breaks the grip of this illusion and gains the ability to see the world as it actually is, rather than as the machines wish it to be seen.

This is a good analogy to what we experience with ego.

We construct identities, and these creations become so powerful that their version of reality takes over. We become convinced that true reality is the one constructed by ego. This construction is filled with separation, fear, and dissatisfaction. If we manage to break through the illusion of ego, we have the chance to see the world as it actually is rather than as ego wants it to be seen.

Our constructed identities are amazing creations. We will always carry these identities with us. The goal is not to eliminate or remove these identities. The goal is to understand them and recognize their place within the whole.

Ego will die when we die. Before that time, we have the challenge of living with ego but not being overtaken by it. We want ego to function without demanding that we believe ego is who we actually are. If we can do this, we will avoid a great deal of fear and dissatisfaction.

When we become adept at recognizing ego, an interesting thing happens. Ego begins to calm down. Once it is discovered, it becomes shy.

For most of my life, I was focused primarily on the constructed aspects of myself. I was so focused on the constructed that I knew very little about the unconstructed. Occasionally, I felt its pull. This pull would exert itself when I was in nature, in quiet contemplation, or so deeply immersed in an experience that I lost myself.

Notice the way our language works here!

When you "lose yourself" within an experience, what is the self that is lost?

And what is found?

Some of the most enjoyable and important moments of our lives occur when we lose ourselves.

At those times, we feel we naturally belong. And our freedom hasn't been diminished.

The maturation process includes the emergence of ego. Ego allows us to recognize ourselves as separate beings and establish identities.

The maturation process may also come to include understanding that our identities are not what we thought they were. It sounds odd, but the challenge is to disidentify with your constructed identity. Your constructed identity is something you have made, not who you are.

> Your constructed identity is something you have made, not who you are.

You have made your constructed identity "the same as you," but it isn't *actually* the same as you. When this becomes clear, you realize you are not who you thought you were.

Who is the creator of your constructed identity?

If you are not who you think you are, then who, or what, are you?

WhoWhatWhere are you?

Ayekah?

KEY TAKEAWAYS

+ Ego is the process of identity construction.
+ Ego disrupts our sense of freedom and belonging.
  ◦ Ego disrupts freedom by distorting its meaning.
  ◦ Ego disrupts belonging by insisting that the unity consciousness we experienced as infants doesn't exist. Ego tells us that separation is the only reality.
+ With the perception of a separate identity and body, there arises the fear of harm.
+ Ego keeps us safe by scanning the world for potential dangers. Ego lives in a perpetual state of fear.
+ It is ego's nature to be dissatisfied with the status quo. This dissatisfaction can spur positive behavior. But egoic consciousness insists on constant dissatisfaction.
+ When egoic, separation consciousness is in charge, unity consciousness can't be experienced. On the other hand, unity consciousness is capable of embracing and including egoic consciousness.
+ The maturation process includes the development of ego. The maturation process may come to include awareness that ego's constructed identity is something you have made, not who you are.
+ If you are not who you thought you were, then who are you?

Two Types of Consciousness

	Unity Consciousness	Egoic, Separation, Consciousness
First appearance	When consciousness begins	Around four months old
Adjectives	Unity; Unified; Unconstructed; Unconditioned	Separate; Separation; Constructed; Conditioned
Character	Unafraid; Content; Accepting	Afraid; Dissatisfied; Resisting
Key phrases	I am free; I belong; Expanding human love and creativity is part of the world's perfection	I want to be free; I want to belong; The world is broken and filled with problems
Final appearance	Unknown	At death

Chapter 3

The Negative Path

The soul grows by subtraction, not addition.
　　　　　—Attributed to Henry David Thoreau

It's DIFFICULT TO DISCOVER WHO you are if you think you already know.

Without fully realizing it, I assumed I was my thoughts, emotions, and my physical body. As long as I thought I knew who I was, I couldn't loosen the ties with my constructed identity.

Famous theologians, such as Maimonides and Aquinas,[1] adopted what became known as the "negative path." Rather than say what God was, they preferred to say what God was not. In their view, the biggest obstacle to understanding God was misunderstanding.

The same is true for people. The biggest obstacle to understanding who you are is getting past the misunderstandings. To understand who you are, it is helpful to understand who you are not.

The ancient Hindu meditation technique of *neti neti,* "not this not this," puts this idea into practice. *Neti neti* meditation consists of noticing what arises in the mind and then acknowledging that it is something other than the deepest truth of who we are.

"Is this thing I can identify the deepest reality? What about this other thing?"

"*Neti neti.* Not this, not this."

The Hindu sage Ramana Maharshi taught that after realizing all the things we aren't, we are left with who we are. But to be effective in uncovering who we are, the realization of who we aren't needs to penetrate beyond the merely intellectual. It needs to become a deep understanding.

> After realizing all the things we aren't, we are left with who we are.

Our body's systems keep us alive and functioning, but they don't define who we are. For example, your digestive system is within you, but the essence of who you are won't be found by examining your digestive system. If you don't identify the essence of who you are with your digestive system, you have already taken one step along the path of *neti neti*.

Our thoughts and feelings are often compelling and attention grabbing. But are these thoughts and feelings who we truly are? Or are they like the body's other systems—phenomena that take place within us but don't define us?

For years, I identified myself with my thoughts. I was out of touch with my body. I responded to its occasional demands, but I related to my body primarily as a vehicle to move my head from place to place. Still, I knew that without my body, my mind wouldn't function. Although my body was secondary to my mind, both were integral to my understanding of who I was.

I viewed emotions as real and important. I knew it was a virtue to be openhearted and compassionate. But I viewed emotions as irrational, and I didn't want the whims of the heart to overshadow the wisdom that arose from reason.

Still, although I placed greater trust in my thoughts, I often experienced powerful emotions. These emotions vied with my thoughts to assert themselves as the most essential truth of who I was. My emotions were uninterested in being subjugated to ideas of what I *should* be feeling.

I experienced a division between my body, thoughts, and emotions. As is the case for many clergy (and academics) ideas, opinions, and beliefs became overly important. I thought "the life of the mind" was the life that mattered.

It is embarrassing to admit, but part of my initial attraction to rabbinic life was the opportunity to lead people to "correct" ideas about God and religion. I thought that correct ideas would lead to correct behaviors. By shifting people's beliefs, I thought I could increase kindness and compassion in the world.

During my years as a congregational rabbi, I came to see that a person's ideas about God, and about religion in general, often had little correlation with kindness or compassion. The ideas, opinions, and beliefs that I thought were so important turned out to be of less value than I had assumed. But I didn't yet know of a different approach.

I was like the young fish in a story told by David Foster Wallace:

> *There are these two young fish swimming along,*
> *and they happen to meet an older fish swimming the*
> *other way, who nods at them and says, "Morning,*
> *boys. How's the water?" And the two young fish*
> *swim on for a bit, and then eventually one of them*
> *looks over at the other and goes, "What the hell is*
> *water?"*[2]

I didn't realize that I identified myself with my thoughts. Nor did I realize that I had created divisions between my mind and body and my thoughts and emotions. I was too immersed in this identity to be able to recognize it.

Are You Your Emotions?

If we have an accelerated heart rate, we might interpret this as nervousness, excitement, fear, or falling in love. These interpretations exert influence on our bodies, which in turn influence our minds. Our bodies reinforce our interpretations, creating an internal loop. But the interpretations of our physical symptoms aren't always reliable.

For example, if you had asked me about my emotional state when I was parenting young children, I might have told you that I was stressed. Looking back, I recognize that I was sleep deprived. But when evaluating how I felt, I interpreted "tired" as "stressed." Although being tired certainly increases stress, the misinterpretation of my physical symptoms caused me to think about how I could reduce stressors in my life, rather than how I could increase sleep.[3]

Moreover, cultures have learned to give different interpretations to physical states. These interpretations affect the body, leading to cultural variation of emotional experiences. For example, Tahitians don't have a word for "sadness." In a situation where you might feel sadness, a Tahitian is more likely to feel ill. Russians don't have words for "excited" or "awkward." And there are plenty of examples of emotional states that exist in other cultures for which there are no English words.

If you want to shift your emotions, you can put on a beloved piece of music. Or you can read the news of the day. These emotional shifts can take place while sitting in a kitchen chair, with no substantive change in your external environment. In this way, emotions are a physical manifestation of our thoughts (e.g., reading the news) and experiences (e.g., listening to music).

Emotions are unreliable interpretations, which vary from culture to culture, of physical symptoms. They are manifestations in the body of thoughts and experiences and can be easily manipulated.

Emotions are something we have, not what we are.

Are You Your Thoughts?

Schools socialize us to identify ourselves with our thoughts. Good students are those capable of good thinking. The world of school tells us that thinking abilities determine worth and value. If you went to school during the first decades of your life, you received this kind of early socialization, and it may still be exerting a powerful influence on you.

Thoughts are more like other biological systems than we often realize. The mind secretes thoughts the way glands secrete hormones. If you believe you control your thoughts, try to stop thinking. Put on a timer and think no thoughts for sixty seconds. If you're like most people, you won't last even a few moments before a thought shows up.

Some of your thoughts are probably unhelpful and unwanted. If you were able to eliminate those thoughts, you would have done so a long time ago.

True, with practice, we can exert some control over our thoughts. But we can also do this with our heart rate, respiration rate, and the body's other systems. Complete control is far out of reach.

You are not in control of your thoughts. And whatever society may say, your value is not based on your IQ, your ability to perform well on exams, or any other measure of your thinking prowess.

The nature of thought itself encourages us to conclude that our true identity can be found within thought. Thought thinks that everything else functions in the service of thought.

Imagine the stomach trying to figure out the meaning of the other bodily systems. To accomplish its tasks, the stomach needs the circulatory system to pump blood. From the perspective of the stomach, the heart exists to enable the digestive system to function.

Now imagine the stomach trying to figure out the meaning of thinking. When the stomach becomes too empty it sends signals that it should be refilled. These signals are translated into the thought "I am hungry." Thought can now take over and accomplish the important task of finding and eating food. From the perspective of the stomach, thought exists to enable the digestive system to function.

From the perspective of the stomach, everything that goes on within you serves digestion. Indeed, from the perspective of each part of your body, everything else exists to serve that particular part.

Our thoughts and emotions play a similar game with us. Our thoughts and emotions tell us that all other aspects of our existence occur for the sake of enabling our thoughts and emotions.

Thought tells us that thought is paramount.

It is difficult for us to ignore this message. To do so, we would need to be in touch with a conscious aspect of ourselves that exists independently of our thoughts. If we try to locate this aspect of our being by thinking, thought will immediately reassert its imagined role as the pinnacle of our existence. It will insist that the purpose of whatever else exists is to serve thought.

Once we recognize that we don't control our thoughts, the question of who or what *is* in control remains.

Are You Your Body?

A close examination of your body will reveal many component parts. Many of these parts are necessary for your survival, but none of these component parts suggest that the body carries your identity. Your identity can't be found in your hair, feet, hands, or kidneys. Thought, and a poor understanding of biology, might want to claim that your identity can be found in your brain. But this is just another example of thought thinking that you are your thoughts.

You may have the thought that you are the sum total of your biological systems, thoughts, and emotions. But this is yet another thought.

It is a theory of being, not an experience of being.

As such, it is ego working to keep its constructed identity in control. Getting caught up in the web of thought stops you from discovering who you really are.

Your emotions, thoughts, and body appear to be connected to this thing called "you," but none of them are equivalent to it. Your body, thoughts, and emotions change drastically during your lifetime. Thoughts and emotions can shift over the course of a few moments. Yet regardless of the body's changes, or the particular thoughts and emotions you have at any moment, you are always you.

If you can't be defined by your thoughts and emotions, then who, or what, are you?

And if you can't be defined by your body, it is fair to ask "where," or on what plane, your existence is taking place. At first glance, it seems that our essential identity is intrinsically tied to our physical selves. But can we be absolutely certain that this is the case?

WhoWhatWhere are you?

Not your body. Not your thoughts. Not your emotions. *Neti neti.* Not this, not this.

In the next chapter, we will begin to explore what we are.

Key Takeaways

- You are not your thoughts; thoughts are something you have.
- You are not your emotions; emotions are something you have.
- You are not your body; your body is something you have.
- You are not your possessions, accomplishments, or mistakes.
- You are not the sum total of your thoughts, emotions, experiences, bodily systems, memories, possessions, accomplishments, mistakes, and so on.
- What is this being that has thoughts, emotions, and a body?

Chapter 4

The End of Seeking

*Wisdom tends to grow in proportion to one's awareness
of one's ignorance.*
—Father Anthony de Mello

FOR MANY YEARS I WAS a spiritual seeker. I was seeking transcendent meaning, purpose, and wisdom, which I associated with God.

As a spiritual seeker, I occasionally experienced altered states of consciousness. Sometimes these altered states showed up as a result of prayer or meditation. And sometimes, they appeared spontaneously. These experiences were very pleasant and gave me a clear sense that I wasn't alone in the universe. But after the experiences passed, I would continue my seeking.

I have come to recognize that my seeking contained a fundamental error. I am not alone in having made this error.

Moses overcomes this error on Mt. Sinai.

In Exodus chapter 33, Moses tells God that he can't continue leading the Israelites through the desert unless God's essence is revealed to Moses in a new and different way. Moses's prior spiritual experiences, as profound as they were, were not enough to sustain him.

Moses says to God: "Please, show yourself to me!"[1]

Apparently, the burning bush, ten plagues, parting of the sea, and the Ten Commandments were not enough for Moses. Altered states and spiritual experiences can be very powerful, but they don't guarantee an end to spiritual seeking.

When I was in spiritual seeking mode, I too wanted God to reveal God's self to me. I imagined that intimacy with God would quell all my doubts about how to live.

God tells Moses that his request will be granted, that God will make "all My goodness pass before you."[2]

But God also tells Moses:

> *You cannot see My face, for a person cannot see*
> *Me and live… I shall put you in the cleft of the rock*
> *and shield you with My hand until I have passed by.*
> *And I will take away My hand and you will see My*
> *back, but My face will not be seen.*[3]

God will *reveal* God's self to Moses. But God will also be *concealed* from Moses.

In Exodus chapter 34, God makes good on the promise of chapter 33. Moses is in a protected spot on Mt. Sinai, and God appears to him. Exodus chapter 34 describes this intimate meeting between God and Moses.

Understanding what happened in this meeting requires a close look at the biblical text. In particular, it requires a close look at the pronouns.

In translating this passage, I have placed pronouns in bold for emphasis.

> YHWH[4] *came down in a cloud, and* **he** *stood with* **him** *there;* **he** *called the name YHWH. YHWH passed across* **his** *face, and* **he** *called out YHWH, YHWH.*[5]

Let's take a close look at the pronouns:

> *YHWH came down in a cloud, and* **he** *stood with* **him** *there.*

Which pronoun refers to Moses and which to YHWH? Because there are no capital letters in Hebrew, it's impossible to tell.[6] Since "he stood with him" means "they stood together," it doesn't matter which pronoun refers to Moses and which to YHWH. However, a level of pronoun confusion has been introduced. This pronoun confusion becomes intensified in what follows.

> **he** *called the name YHWH.*

Who called the name YHWH? Was this God, calling the name YHWH? Or was this Moses calling out to God? The confusion is never resolved.

> *YHWH passed across* **his** *face…*

This is clear. "His" refers to Moses's face.

> *and **he** called out YHWH, YHWH* (va'yikra
> YHWH YHWH).

Who called out?

Did Moses call out YHWH? Or did God call out
YHWH?

It's impossible to know.

On its own, *va'yikra* means "he called out" or "it called
out." In context, *"va'yikra YHWH YHWH"* has three
possible meanings:

1. YHWH called out: "YHWH"
2. He [Moses] called out: "YHWH YHWH"
3. He/it [YHWH] called out: "YHWH YHWH"

If there were only one YHWH, it would be natural
to assume that the speaker was God. Doubling the name
YHWH in this passage helps to keep the meaning of the
pronouns obscure. This is the only place the Bible uses
the phrase *"va'yikra YHWH YHWH."*

At this peak moment of the relationship between God and
Moses, did the biblical author(s)[7] get sloppy, making it hard
for us to figure out who is speaking and who is listening?

I don't think so. I believe the pronoun confusion is
intentional and carefully constructed. It starts in verse
five and is carried over to verse six. The text is telling us

that Moses and YHWH are simultaneously the speaker and the listener.

In these verses, Moses, who has begged God to "please show Yourself to me!" finally finds what he was seeking. What he finds is that God is not separate from Moses. They are two sides of a coin.

Moses the seeker disappears in the recognition that he is what he was seeking.

A sole went out in search of the foot. It wandered far and wide, hoping that perhaps the foot would be discovered in a different location. It called out to the foot, "Please, reveal yourself to me!" hoping to receive a response. The sole practiced walking meditations. It hoped that these meditations might one day cause the foot to appear.

Eventually, the sole became so exhausted from its efforts that it stopped all its travels, meditations, and prayers. The poor sole was tired and confused. It wasn't even certain that it was still a sole.

Then, in a moment of insight, it recognized that the sole and the foot are one.

Once this recognition occurred, the sole would never again go in search of the foot.

Every day on her way to market, the great Sufi mystic Rabiya passed Hassan sitting outside the door of the mosque. Hassan was devout. He prayed aloud with great intensity. "God, please open the door! Let me in!"

One morning Rabiya saw that Hassan was crying. Tears were rolling down his cheeks, and he was shouting again and again, "Open the door! Let me in! Why don't You listen? Why don't You hear my prayers?"

Rabiya approached Hassan, shook him, and said, "Stop all this nonsense! The door is open—in fact you are already in!"

That moment became a moment of revelation. Looking into Rabiya's eyes, Hassan said, "If you hadn't come, I would have called to God my whole life! For years I have been doing this—where were you before? You must have seen me crying out and praying."

Rabiya said, "Truth can only be said at a certain moment, in a certain space, in a certain context. I was waiting for the right moment. Today it arrived. If I had spoken to you yesterday, you would have felt irritated. You may have even become angry. You may have told me, 'You have disturbed my prayer!'—and it is not right to disturb anybody's prayer."

Rabiya said, "I had wanted to tell you this many times. 'Hassan, don't be a fool, the door is open—in fact, you are already in!' But I had to wait for the right moment."

Simha Bunim (1765–1827) was a famous Polish rabbi. People would travel great distances to study with him. When the travelers would first arrive, he would tell them this story:

> *Rabbi Isaac of Kraków was very devout and very poor. One night he had a dream that under the bridge that leads to the king's palace in Prague, a great treasure was buried. When the dream recurred for the third time, Rabbi Isaac set out for Prague.*
>
> *When he arrived at the bridge, he saw that it was guarded day and night. He was afraid to dig, but he kept returning to the bridge every morning. He spent all his waking hours in Prague walking around the bridge until one day the captain of the guard politely asked him what he was doing there.*
>
> *Rabbi Isaac told him about his dream and the great distance he had traveled.*
>
> *The captain of the guard laughed and said: "That's the craziest story I have ever heard! You traveled here based on a dream! Let me tell you, if dreams were reliable, I would have long ago left my post here to travel to Kraków. I once had a dream that told me to go there and to dig for treasure under the stove in the house of a man named Isaac. Can you imagine! I would have had to go to every house in Kraków, where half of the men are named Isaac, and ask every Isaac if I could dig under his stove to look for treasure."*
>
> *And he laughed again.*

Rabbi Isaac traveled home and dug up the treasure from under his stove.

Rabbi Simha Bunim would tell those who had traveled to study with him:

Take this story to heart. There is a treasure you cannot find no matter how far you travel. It is a great treasure, which may be called the fulfillment of existence.

The place where this treasure can be found is the place where you stand.

The fundamental error I made, and that virtually all spiritual seekers make, is the assumption that there is an "I" who desires a relationship with God. This "I" is nothing but a clever construction.

The misunderstanding is that I am "here," and the God I seek is somewhere "over there." But I am not "here," and God is not "there." This misunderstanding keeps the spiritual seeker searching for buried treasure.

The altered states I experienced during my spiritual seeking days were suggesting a different truth. But each time these states subsided, I would return to my normal consciousness and repeat the fundamental error. I would assume that my constructed identity was who I was and that this constructed identity had experienced an altered state.

This was wrong. During these altered states, my constructed identity moved to the background. When my constructed identity receded, I was able to encounter my unconstructed identity.

My constructed identity was an impediment to these experiences, but it thought it was their subject and their creator.

> My constructed identity was an impediment to these experiences, but it thought it was their subject and their creator.

God's Name

At the end of his seeking, Moses finds out that he is not separate from YHWH, that they are two sides of the same coin. As Moses's constructed "I" moves from foreground to background, the coin turns from the Moses side to the YHWH side.

What is found on this side of the coin?

Efforts to describe this side of the coin are as likely to distort as they are to illuminate. Attempting a description is similar to the challenge of describing the color red to a blind person. At best, we might say that red is like the warmth of a fire, or the color of rage. These descriptions don't do red justice and might even lead to greater confusion.

The biblical author(s) came up with a creative solution to this difficulty: God's four-letter name, YHWH.

The Name YHWH

There are many words for God in Hebrew. For example, *el* and *elohim* both mean God. "God" is a concept. People can have different ideas about what God is, whether God exists, and so on.

YHWH does not mean God.

YHWH is a proper name. My name is Dan. God's name is YHWH.

Hebrew words typically contain three-letter roots. The root of YHWH is the last three letters: *h, w, h* or hey, vav, hey. These three letters are the root of the verb "to be."

The first letter of God's name is the letter *y*, or yod. The letter yod in this location signifies the third person masculine singular "he," or the impersonal third person, "it."

This particular construction of the verb "to be," YHWH, is a hopeless conflation of tenses. The word is a combination of how this verb looks in its past, present, and future forms. It is impossible to say what tense is indicated. An attempt at translating this word might look something like "Is Was Will Be."[8]

The challenge of the translation is to bring all tenses to mind without correctly referring to any of them. Is Was-WillBe correctly refers to all tenses. It is a usable translation even though it loses some of the playfulness of the original Hebrew.

The word YHWH can't be pronounced. To make the name pronounceable, some people add vowels. For example, YaHWeH contains an added *a* and *e*. These added vowels don't exist in the biblical text. They are additions to make pronunciation possible.

The fact that YHWH can't be pronounced is not due to a religious restriction against saying the name out loud. It is unpronounceable because…just try pronouncing YHWH. My attempts at pronouncing YHWH sound something like breathing, or like wind passing through the trees.

Putting this together we see that:

+ YHWH is not a concept. YHWH is a proper name.
+ YHWH is a verb.
+ YHWH is an impossible form of the verb "to be." It means something like IsWasWillBe.
+ YHWH can't be pronounced. If you try to pronounce it, it might evoke the sound of the air, or breath.

The meaning of the name YHWH is hiding, but it is hiding in plain sight.

> *You cannot see My face, for a person cannot see Me and live.*[9]

When Moses's constructed "I" recedes, and the proverbial coin turns away from the Moses side, Moses finds YHWH, IsWasWillBe, pure being.

Moses's new understanding was more than an intellectual breakthrough. Moses experiences enlightenment. He awakens to a new understanding. "Seeing the light" is a phrase often used to describe this awakening.

He didn't just see the light. He internalized the light. His transformation was so powerful that

> *When Aaron and all the Israelites saw Moses, his face radiated light, and they were afraid to approach him. Moses called to them, and they returned to him.*[10]

As long as this remains merely a description of Moses's experience, or an interesting and clever theory about God, it won't help you.

However, if these words prompt experience and discovery, then transformation becomes possible. The end of the seeker is in sight.

It is a mistake to think that the treasure of enlightenment is available only to someone like Moses and only after a lifetime of spiritual practice. This treasure is not in a faraway place. It can be found in this moment and in the place where you stand.

In fact, the treasure of enlightenment can *only* be found in the present moment and in the place where you stand.

Ego is quite capable of using humility for its own purposes.

The voice of doubt that denies the possibility that enlightenment is available to you right here, and right now, is the voice of ego. It is doing its best to stay in charge. Ego is quite capable of using humility for its own purposes.

Enlightenment may not be exactly what you think it is. Rather than rely on preconceived notions of enlightenment, remain open to experience and let it be your guide.

There are many paths to discovery, and not all paths work for all people. I will introduce three paths that have spurred my own discovery. Perhaps at least one of these paths will help you as well.

Each of these paths can bring you to an experience of enlightenment. It doesn't require years of practice. It only requires your full and complete devotion in the immediate moment.

The Path of Inquiry

You are not your thoughts. But your thoughts have the potential to lead you to who you are.

Sit quietly for a moment with your eyes closed and attempt to locate the place within you from which your thoughts arise.

Do this now, for as long or short a period as you like.

What did you experience?

Many people report that when they look for the place where thought arises, thought itself becomes quiet. It's as if thoughts get shy when they know they are being examined. The process of identity construction becomes short-circuited, at least for a moment.

Another common experience is the inability to find the place from which thoughts arise. It seems to be beyond our grasp, just out of reach. This can be experienced as a failure to succeed in the task.

But being unable to locate the place from which thoughts arise may actually be a success. The place where thought arises can't be found with a thought—it precedes thought. We are used to assuming that correct answers must be framed within the realm of thought. This assumption can lead us to discount the experience of quiet invisibility.

If you looked and found "nothing," consider yourself lucky. It is entirely possible that the quiet invisibility you encountered is the essence of your being. This "nothing" that you experienced might just be the place from which thoughts arise and the place they go as they fade away.

> *You will see My back, but My face will not be seen.*

We want to understand ourselves better. We are drawn to quizzes that tell us what Disney character we are or what Harry Potter character we are. These efforts are typically driven by ego. By adding on another layer of identity (e.g., I'm Hermione!), we reinforce the process of identity construction.

Ego's conditioned identity finds the experience of quiet invisibility unsatisfying. If an experience can't be used to strengthen ego's control over our identity, ego will tell us that it is unimportant.

The process of identity construction is not the deepest truth of our being. Identity construction is a layer of mental activity that arises from a deeper place within us.

We are pure being having the experience of constructing identities and living as humans. This is who we are. With this recognition, the importance of ego diminishes. And many of the things that made us unhappy fall away.

The phrases "I am sad" and "I am happy" speak in the language of identity construction. These phrases imply that emotional states are who we are. For the quiet invisibility that you may have just encountered—for pure being—the experience might be more like "sadness is present" or "happiness is present."

For pure being, emotional states like sadness and happiness come and go. They don't define us, and they are not a full description of our experience. Even when "sadness is present," there are many other things present as well. When we get stuck in a particular mood, whatever that mood may be, we are most likely stuck in the process of identity construction.

If you want enlightenment to result in an endless puddle of bliss, this might not be what you want to hear. There is no way to live as a human being without experiencing sadness. Sadness and even depression are a part of life. However, it may be possible to avoid getting stuck in a particular state. A particular mood or state can be with you for a long while, but change is in our nature. If you don't identify with the mood, if instead of "*I* am depressed," the experience is "depression is (one thing that is) present," you are less likely to get stuck.

Pure being, if we take the time to get to know it well, is able to take its rightful place and become acknowledged as our essence. In reality, it is our essence whether or not we acknowledge it. And it doesn't require or insist upon being acknowledged. If a person wants to imagine that their constructed identity is the deepest truth of their existence, pure being won't object. One of the ways you can recognize ego is that it wants to argue and provide proofs. Pure being doesn't seem to be interested in arguing for itself.

Take another moment to try to locate the place within you from which thought arises. This time, if you are lucky enough to find nothing, become curious about this nothing.

What does it feel like? What is the nature of this nothing? Is it young? Old? Timeless? Male? Female? Is it Muslim, atheist, Buddhist, Jewish, Christian, agnostic, or some other religion? Is it happy? Sad? Equanimous? Something else?

Spend as much time as you are comfortable exploring the experience of this nothing. Eventually, you will return to the routines of your life. But you can always return to explore again.

Your comfort with exploring this nothing may be related to the level of threat your constructed identity is experiencing. The process of identity construction doesn't want to be displaced as the center of your being. It will do whatever it can to reassert its preeminence. It may try to convince you that the nothing is boring and inconsequential. Or ego may conjure up terrible images of what will happen if it is no longer in charge.

These experiences point to your success. If the process of identity construction is responding defensively, you must be making progress.

The path of inquiry contains many roads. I have suggested a single prompt, "Locate the place from which your thoughts arise," but there are many other ways to access this path. For example, the questions of "What, exactly, is this thing I call life?" and "How did I come to believe what I believe?" and "Who would I be without my beliefs?" might also be helpful to you. All of these questions are a version of the fundamental question "WhoWhatWhere am I?"

Ayekah?

Many questions, if asked with sincerity and curiosity, can lead to the experience of pure being.

It is not by self-realization that humans realize God; it is by God-realization that humans realize self. —Inayat Khan[11]

What you seek is seeking you.—Rumi[12]

The Path of Listening

You are not your emotions. But your emotions have the potential to lead you to who you are.

One of the pillars of the Jewish prayer service is a biblical verse that is directed not to God but to people.

שמ**ע** ישראל יהוה אלהינו יהוה אח**ד**
Listen *(shema)*, Israel, our God, YHWH, is one.[13]

Israel here refers not to a geographic location but to the people Israel who say these words to one another. "Listen, Israel" is an instruction from person to person.

To truly listen requires a quality of attention that is uncompromised by internal commentary. Most of us start formulating our response before someone is done speaking instead of being fully dedicated to listening.

Deep listening implies total openness and receptivity. It is done with the entirety of one's being, not just with the ears. In particular, listen with the heart.

Wherever you are, give yourself a moment to fall into the quiet attention of deep listening. The moment can last for as short, or as long, as you like.

שמ**ע** ישראל יהוה אלהינו יהוה אח**ד**

This verse is often written with two enlarged letters—the last letter of the first word and the last letter of the last word. These two letters form the word *witness*.

Witness consciousness is a phrase sometimes used to describe what lies at the center of our being. Witness consciousness is awareness itself. It notices, witnesses, everything that happens. This witness consciousness is always in the background, observing life even as it participates in living life.

When we engage in deep listening, we access witness consciousness. We become aware of awareness.

Listening in this manner is a type of meditation. It can be done with eyes open or closed, alone or with others.

Listen.

Shema.

The Hebrew word *shema*, "listen," also carries the meaning "obey."

Deep listening will elicit a response. It may be a response of the heart, a verbal response, or a response that requires action by the hands or feet.

The response to deep listening may or may not be what another person wants or expects. Listening with a quality of total openness and receptivity is not an invitation to be passive. Deep listening will lead to taking appropriate action. But the listening precedes the action. When we don't allow ourselves to listen fully, we are more likely to take actions that are motivated by ego.

Listening with total openness means allowing oneself to be changed, to be called to a response.

Forget about finding your way, you are already that which you are seeking. —Papaji[14]

Whoever knows themselves, knows God.
—Attributed to Yahya ibn Mu'adh al-Razi[15]

The Path of the Body

You are not your body. But your body has the potential to lead you to who you are.

If you ask yourself, "What am I?" thoughts may rush in and create concepts.

If you want an experience of what you are, rather than a concept, the body is an excellent teacher.

+   Rub your hands together for a few moments and then separate them. Feel the energy in your hands. Rub them together again. Draw your hands closer together, though never touching, and then farther apart. Can you feel the energy in your hands?

* Now attempt to feel the energy in your hands without first rubbing them together. If you aren't able to do this, don't worry. Continue to place your attention on your hands, and perhaps eventually you will be able to feel their energy.

* If you are able to feel the energy in your hands, bring your attention to your feet. Just as there is energy in your hands, there is energy in your feet. Place your attention on your feet, attempting to feel their energy.

* If you were able to feel the energy in both your hands and feet, place your attention on the energy of your hands and feet simultaneously. If it helps, you may want to close your eyes.

* If you are able to feel the energy in your hands and feet, keep your attention there, and also bring your attention to the energy around your heart. Keep your focus on these three different areas of energy in the body. How is the energy similar or different in each area? How does the energy shift and change as you watch it? Stay with this exercise for as long or short a time as you are comfortable.

* If you had success with this last exercise, attempt to re-create that success. Keeping

> yourself grounded with the energies of the hands, feet, and heart, allow yourself to feel the energy of your entire body. Notice the differences and similarities between the energies of the feet, legs, hands, arms, pelvis, stomach, chest, back, neck, and head. Notice how the energy of the body changes as you watch it. Stay with this exercise for as long or short a time as you are comfortable.

With practice, you can become more familiar with the energy of your body.

Thoughts provide concepts. The body provides a lived experience of the life within you. If you are able to stay with the *experience* of the body and avoid being pulled into your *ideas* about the body, ego recedes.

What is the nature of this life energy within you? Is it similar or different to the energy of a battery, or electricity? Does it contain a sort of wisdom? Is there a type of awareness at play within the energy of the body? Is this awareness always present? Or is it only present when you place your attention upon it?

When I ask myself these questions, I sense that this awareness is always present. Placing my attention upon it gives me the sense of awareness becoming aware of itself.

But don't take my word for it. Use experience as your guide. Your experience is your true teacher.

You are more sacred than you can ask or imagine!
Deep within you know that your body is a temple
where the Holy Spirit lives. (1 Corinthians 6:19)

That which is the finest essence—this whole
world has that as its self. That is reality. That is
atman (soul). You are that. (Chandogya Upanishad
6.8–16)

Let's return to the name YHWH.

+ YHWH is not a concept. YHWH is a proper
  name.
+ YHWH is a verb.
+ YHWH is an impossible form of the verb "to
  be." It means something like IsWasWillBe.
+ YHWH can't be pronounced. If you try to
  pronounce it, it might evoke the sound of the
  air, or breath.

The meaning of the name YHWH is hiding, but it is
hiding in plain sight.

This description conforms to my experiences when I
follow the paths of inquiry, listening, and the body. What
I have been calling pure being is not a concept. It is active,

moving, and changing, yet it conveys a deep stillness. It is being—not past, present, or future, but all of them and none of them at the same time. It is impossible to adequately describe in words.

The *Tao Te Ching*[16] tells us that "The name that can be named is not the enduring and unchanging name." *Brahman* is a Sanskrit word that points to the unseen essence of everything that exists. *Christ-consciousness* and *Buddha-nature* are terms that point to the unseen aspect of the universe that is manifest within human consciousness. Sufi poets and authors like Rumi and Inayat Khan express similar ideas. There are undoubtedly many other beautiful articulations of similar concepts originating from other cultures and traditions.

Scholars can, and should, draw attention to the ways these words and ideas are distinct from one another. The words and ideas originated within specific cultures. We should expect those cultures to have influenced the way the ideas are expressed. But for the person who has experienced pure being, this conversation among scholars is academic. The attempt to capture the experience in words will necessarily be culturally or religiously specific. The experience itself appears to be universal.

Each of the three paths I have described—the path of inquiry, the path of listening, and the path of the body can lead to an experience of pure being. As you experimented with these paths, did you sense an awake, alive awareness within you move from the background to the foreground? Even if only for a moment? If so, then you had a taste of enlightenment.

If you are like most people, you touched this experience of enlightenment and then returned to your normal way of existing in the world. But enlightened consciousness can develop deeper roots and become a regular way of experiencing life. It is not hard for me to imagine that it could even become the usual way for a person to exist in the world.

Over time, I have become more familiar with this quiet awareness, this no-thing. And although I still spend too much time living and acting from ego, I am much more alert to ego's tricks than I used to be. I regularly experience life from this place of quiet awareness. And I am constantly on guard for when even this perception becomes yet another tool in ego's bag of tricks, which still occurs.

I hope that I become less attached to protecting my constructed identity. This will make room for me to become more aware of the life force that is always operating through me. When I experience life in this fashion, I am calmer, happier, lighter, and more open to giving and receiving love. Eventually, I will die, at which point I expect my constructed identity will disappear forever.

For now, it is enough if you were able to recognize that beneath your constructed identity there lies a different truth about who you really are. Indeed, this is groundbreaking.

Your thoughts and emotions arise from a quiet, alive, nothingness. And it is this quiet, alive, nothingness to which your thoughts and emotions occur.

The words used to describe this aspect of your being all fall short. Life force; nothingness; quiet stillness;

spirit; witness consciousness; unconstructed identity; awareness; Tao; Brahman; God; Christ-consciousness; Buddha-nature; YHWH; pure being. None of the words are adequate. Choose whichever words you prefer and ignore the rest.

Ayekah? WhoWhatWhere are you?

You may or may not be aware of it, but you are the life force itself.

I sense that the life force that is me is the same as the life force that is you. This same life force animates the trees, grasses, birds, and everything else that exists. This life force takes on different forms, but it is unified, it is one.

I experience pure being as having its own intelligence, life, and wisdom. In this way, it is like a person.

YHWH is a proper name. It answers the question, "*Who* are you?"

Because the same life force animates the trees and the grasses, the word *what* sometimes seems more appropriate than *who*.

YHWH is a verb. It answers the question "*What* are you?"

And because this life force is me, but not confined to me, the question of "where" is limited only by my experience. It is easy to say "I am everywhere," but for me, this statement is usually conceptual rather than experiential. I prefer to dwell with the question, "WhoWhatWhere are you?" and allow responses to emerge naturally, nonverbally. When I engage in this practice, I will often sense that my being, and all of being, are the same.

YHWH, IsWasWillBe, is timeless and all time. YHWH cannot be geographically confined. It answers the question *"Where* are you?"

WhoWhatWhere are you? IsWasWillBe.

The internal Copernican revolution[17] is that the constructed you doesn't become aware. It is awareness that is aware. And it always has been. You are this quiet, alive awareness.

The belief that your constructed identity is the true you is misguided. Your constructed identity is a game being played by awareness.

A common, clever, and dangerous trick of ego is to appropriate this insight for its own purposes. The trick is dangerous because there are few things more annoying than egos using spiritual insights to prop themselves up. I know, because I have years of experience doing exactly this. The professional identity of "rabbi" is an open invitation to commit this error. Too often, I eagerly accepted the invitation. I am always on guard against this trick of ego, fearing that I might be falling for it yet again.

To help avoid falling for this trick, keep in mind:

+ Realizing that you are awareness itself doesn't make you better than anyone else. Everyone else is awareness itself too.
+ "You" aren't enlightened. The belief that "you" experienced a sense of enlightenment

is mistaken. It shows that the truth of your experience hasn't yet been fully internalized. This belief is a sign that there is another level of understanding waiting to be discovered. Use this sign as a motivation to go deeper.

If you see the illusion, you are enlightened. But if you think that you are enlightened, you are in the illusion. —Papaji

If you want to know yourself, make it your mission to become on ever more intimate terms with this awesome, quiet awareness.

Realizing and internalizing WhoWhatWhere you are brings about a fundamental shift of identity.

When your old, constructed identity is no longer capable of pretending to be the sole truth of who you are, the spiritual fun can truly begin.

Awareness
Consciousness
Unconstructed identity
Nothing that is everything
Pure being
Quiet stillness
YHWH
Witness

SEEKING
YEARNING
LONGING

Ego
Separation
I want; I think; I feel
Constructed identity
Fear
Dissatisfaction

AWAKENED CONSCIOUSNESS

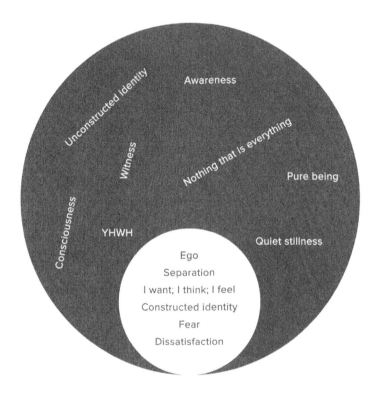

Seeking, yearning, and longing have fallen away.

PART 2

LIFE WITHOUT
SEEKING

Chapter 5

Feeling Better

Truth exists; only falsehood has to be invented.
—Georges Braque

MY SPIRITUAL AWAKENING HAD A clear before and after. Before awakening, I was seeking an intimacy with God. After awakening, I couldn't convince myself to seek for what I already was.

Initially, I could only access awakened consciousness in silence and with my eyes closed. When my eyes were open, distractions flooded in. And when I spoke, I would lose connection with conscious awareness. Over time, I have learned to maintain my connection to conscious awareness when speaking and with eyes open.

I have always enjoyed taking walks and appreciating the beauty of the natural world. Taking walks after awakening, I sometimes experienced that my eyes were doing the looking, but there was something else seeing through them. I was taking awareness out for a stroll.

This experience was very powerful. It was a fundamental shift of identity, and it resulted in a newfound happiness and wonder. I was filled with joy, contentment, and love.

And then the experience went away.

At first, I wondered whether the experience of awakened consciousness would ever return. When it did return, it was only to disappear again. I cycled in and out of awakened consciousness. I couldn't predict when it would show up and when it would go away.

I still move between awakened and unawakened consciousness. For the past few years, awakened consciousness has always been available. But even though awakened consciousness is available, I don't always access it.

My lifelong tendency to identify with my thoughts and emotions is still with me. But there has been a change. As opposed to my younger years, I eventually recognize what's happening. Once ego's identification process is fully recognized, it shifts. The witness that observes ego at work moves from the background to the foreground. And ego's efforts to add layers of identity moves from foreground to background. Ego doesn't disappear, but it ceases to be in control.

I know I should eat well and exercise regularly. When I do, I feel better and enjoy life more. But I sometimes eat poorly and forgo exercise. This tells me there is a level of knowledge that I haven't yet attained. If my knowledge had become true understanding, then I would always eat well and exercise regularly.

Similarly, I am capable of living from conscious awareness. When I do, I feel better and enjoy life more. But I don't always do it.

This tells me that my knowledge of who I am is still in process. There is a level of understanding that I have not yet attained. As my knowledge gradually becomes true understanding, I imagine I will live more of my life from conscious awareness.

When it comes to advanced spirituality, I am still a beginner.

Providing an answer to Who What Where you are is different from living the answer. Living the answer means living from conscious awareness rather than from constructed identity.

Ego is still very much alive within me. My challenge is to make use of ego's contributions when they are valuable and then put ego back in its appropriate place. But it is the nature of ego to always want control.

Egoic consciousness and unity consciousness are both part of human experience. The reality of unity doesn't negate the reality of separation.

Although unity doesn't negate separation, it does *precede* separation. Unity consciousness existed within us before we perceived separation.

And unity consciousness should take *precedence*. Unity consciousness perceives truths that are hidden by ego's dogmatic insistence on separation.

This can be illustrated by looking outside and seeing something growing out of the ground with leaves, branches, and a trunk. You can name this thing, and by naming it, you experience the satisfaction of understanding what it is. It is a tree.

But does the word *tree* help you understand what you are seeing?

The tree has roots that penetrate the soil. Nutrients from the soil are being extracted by the roots and moving through the tree. Photosynthesis is processing light from the sun and turning it into food. The tree is taking in carbon dioxide and emitting oxygen.

Where are the borders and boundaries between soil, atmosphere, sun, and tree?

The borders and boundaries exist within the words we use. The word *tree* is descriptive and often helpful. But the word *tree* obscures the fact that the tree isn't a separate entity. What we call a tree is part of a grand unity that extends below the ground and into the sky.

By using words that call attention to separateness, we diminish our ability to perceive unity. The word *tree* encourages us to perceive separateness and masks the interconnectedness of all life. The existence of the tree as an independent entity is an illusory concept created by human beings.

When I say that a tree is an illusory concept, I don't mean that the tree you see doesn't exist. Unity doesn't negate separation, and the tree can and should be appreciated for itself. But the human-created concept of "tree" masks the deeper reality of unity. When we break unity into separate parts, we imagine those separate parts have independent existence. This is an error, so the word *illusion* is apt.[1]

This is understandable when applied to the concept of "tree," but let's take it a step further and apply the same thinking to the concept of "me."

We think of ourselves as separate beings. But just as we asked about the tree, where are the borders and boundaries between you and other people, earth, plants, animals, atmosphere, and sun? Are you different from the tree because you are mobile and extract nutrients from the earth without using roots? Are you different because instead of taking in carbon dioxide and emitting oxygen you do the opposite? You don't engage in photosynthesis, but without the energy of the sun, you too wouldn't exist.

When you name yourself as a separate being, you obscure the truth of unity. It isn't just that you couldn't sustain yourself if you were the only thing that existed. The idea that you have independent existence is an illusion. That which exists is both within you and outside of you.

The borders between the existence within you and outside of you are concepts. On one level, they are descriptive, but on another level, they aren't real. Without words, you might perceive life in the way that you probably perceived it before you acquired language. You might perceive the world as a unity, with no separation between you and everything else.

Which perception is true? The perception of separateness or the perception of unity? The answer is that both are true. But separateness is a perception we impose upon the world. Unity is the more fundamental truth.

Modern science has reinforced this insight. Science tells us that everything is made up of the same basic substance. This basic substance changes shape and shows up as rocks, streams, grasses, flowers, dogs, cats, humans, air, stars, planets, and so on. Existence shows up in infinite forms.

From the standpoint of existence, there is no hierarchy. When the unity of all existence takes the form of a flea, it doesn't smack itself on the wrist for not having shown up as a dog. From the smallest form to the most complex, it is all the same unity. The life force of the universe brought you into existence and continues to animate your being. And this same life force brings each blade of grass into existence and keeps it alive.

A mature perception of unity (vs. the perception of unity we had as babies) is aware of the differences between a person and a blade of grass. In a mature perception of unity, the infinite variety of forms is appreciated and enjoyed. But many people fool themselves into thinking that the variety is all that exists; that beyond separateness, there is no unity. This is an illusion.

This illusion serves egoic consciousness. As we begin to internalize the reality that we aren't separate from one another, the process of identity construction loosens its grip. But be careful…the process of identity construction will use the *thought* of unity as another arrow in its quiver. "*I'm* so wise and special, *I* understand that everything is one!"

Unity eliminates a certain type of hierarchy. You are more complex than a blade of grass. This complexity allows you to perform tasks like walking and speaking. But you and the blade of grass are two forms of the same essential stuff.

A true recognition of unity will lead to humility rather than a sense of superiority.

It would be true for a leaf to say "I am a leaf" and for a branch to say "I am a branch." It would also be true for both leaf and branch to say "I am a tree." And as we have seen, it would be true for a tree to say "I am earth, air, water, and sun." These truths exist simultaneously, they do not negate each other.

Similarly, it is true for you to say "I am me" but it is also true for you to say "I am earth, air, water, and sun." The concepts of "me" and "tree" help us speak about the world, but they obscure as much as if not more than they reveal.

The tree is living its life. It's also true to say that life is living the tree.

You are living your life. But on a deeper level, life is living you.

Moving Beyond Ego's Control

Life doesn't conform to ego's preconceived notions. Instead of following ego's insistence that life is supposed to be a certain way, we need to acknowledge that life is what it is.

When ego is no longer in control, everything doesn't suddenly become wonderful. Instead, ego's preoccupation with keeping us dissatisfied is exposed and replaced by an embrace of truth.

When I write about truth, I am not making a claim about ideas. At best, ideas carry partial truths. And communicating partial truths implies the likelihood of communicating partial falsehoods.

By truth I mean reality. Truth is what is, not what I imagine.

The Hebrew word for truth, *emet*, is spelled aleph, mem, tav. These three letters are the first, middle, and last letters of the Hebrew alphabet. The Jewish sages taught that truth is all-encompassing. There is a vast broadness to truth. Truth includes everything from A to Z.[2]

The first letter of *emet* is aleph. In Jewish lore, aleph, the first letter of the alphabet, signifies that which lies at the beginning of everything. Aleph signifies YHWH, pure being, the nothing that is everything.

The nothing that is everything precedes thought. It is the place from which thought arises and the witness to which thought occurs. If we try to arrive at truth using only thought, then we are leaving the YHWH element out. And truth can't be captured by using thought alone.

Truth, *emet*, without the aleph, leaves the letters mem and tav, spelling *met*, the Hebrew word for dead.

Loving truth isn't about preaching certainty. Loving truth requires embracing uncertainty.

> Loving truth requires embracing uncertainty.

Truth, being all-encompassing, means everything that is. It includes elements of reality that exist outside the realm of thoughts and ideas. YHWH, IsWasWillBe, and truth, containing the beginning, middle, and end, are related to one another.

Truth, like YHWH, is at once a mystery and plainly evident. Truth, reality, what is, is staring us in the face at every moment.

In Buddhist tradition, Mara is the demon who distracts humans from spiritual development.

> *One day Mara was traveling through the villages of India with his attendants. He saw a man doing walking meditation whose face was lit up with wonder. The man had just discovered something on the ground in front of him.*
>
> *Mara's attendant asked what the man had discovered. Mara replied, "A piece of truth." "Doesn't it bother you when someone finds a piece of truth?" the attendant asked. "No," Mara replied. "Right after the discovery, they usually make a belief out of it."*

One instance in which I made a belief out of truth occurred when I first discovered that my previously presumed identity was actually an elaborate construction. I turned this truth into a belief. Instead of believing I was Dan, I believed I was pure being. The ego creation known as Dan was of little use or interest to me.

I thought I had made a significant spiritual leap, but I had just replaced one belief with another. When I was on familiar terms with my constructed identity, I believed that was who I was. As I became more familiar with my unconstructed identity, I believed that was who I was. Both beliefs kept me from the truth.

There is an element of mystery in the human experience that can't be captured by beliefs. In an effort to penetrate and understand this mystery I am susceptible to creating new beliefs that stop me from embracing the uncertainty contained within truth. My mind wants to conquer uncertainty and make the unknown known. I have had to train my mind to avoid falling into the trap that Mara identified.

> *"Doesn't it bother you when someone finds a piece of truth?" the attendant asked. "No," Mara replied. "Right after the discovery, they usually make a belief out of it."*

As I became familiar with my unconstructed identity, I believed I had solved the mystery of human existence. Over time, I have discovered that the truth is more complicated.

I have had to work on appreciating and honoring ego's ongoing role in my life. The awakening experience was freeing and filled me with contentment. Early on, when ego showed up, conscious awareness was no longer accessible. Because of this, I related to ego as an unwelcome visitor. Gradually, this has changed.

Ego plays an important role, allowing me to function as a human being. It is true that I am the nothing that is everything. But it's also true that I am Dan, a particular human being with a particular background and personality. The challenge for me now is integrating ego and conscious awareness into the whole experience of "me."

The diagrams of unawakened and awakened consciousness at the end of the last chapter provide a graphic illustration of this challenge. When living from ego, the experience is of division. My spiritual seeking was predicated on believing this division was real. I yearned for "something more." But after leaving spiritual seeking, I still created division. I was unable to welcome ego into the totality of my existence without being swallowed up by it.

Over time I have learned that living from conscious awareness includes honoring ego and its identity-producing role without being controlled by it.

If division is present in the form of ego being cast out, then awakened consciousness can't take hold. Yes, it's true that I am pure being. But it's also true that I am this particular being. The interplay between my constructed and unconstructed identities, and the relationship between my existence and all of existence, contain elements of mystery. My life gives me the opportunity to explore this mystery. Thoughts that I have solved the mystery are an indication that I have, yet again, turned truth into a belief.

Much of human emotional activity is devoted to resisting and denying truth. Our attempts to resist and deny truth contribute to our suffering.

I am not suggesting that resisting truth is the only or even the main cause of our suffering. Rather, our attempts to deny truth are a way we *contribute* to our suffering.

We all tell ourselves a series of stories about our lives. Many of the stories we tell ourselves aren't conscious. For example, without being aware of it, I used to tell myself the story that my father would live until at least his late seventies. It was a reasonable story, and as it turns out, I was quite attached to it. But my story wasn't true.

My father died at age sixty-nine. When he died, the story I had been telling myself about his lifespan needed to be discarded. I needed a new story to take its place. In my new story, the true story, my father died at sixty-nine and didn't get to see his grandchildren grow up. I preferred the story where my father lived longer.

I knew my father had died, but I resisted this truth, pushing against it with emotional force. "It's not right! It's not fair! He was supposed to live longer!"

The reality of life appears to be uninterested in our ideas of what is "right" or "fair." Our ideas of what is "supposed to happen" may sometimes come to pass, but even then, reality is rarely an exact copy of what we had imagined.

My father died at sixty-nine. And I needed to adjust to that truth.

My old story, the one I preferred, the one I loved, needed to be discarded. But it is hard to discard something that you love, even if it is only a story. My emotional insistence on "fairness" and what was "supposed to happen" were ways of holding on to my old story, the story I loved.

I didn't like the new story. The true story.

The question for me was which I loved more: my old story or truth? As long as I loved my old story more than truth, more than reality, I was locked in an emotional battle. My resistance to truth kept my old story alive.

Eventually, my love of truth won out.

Was it "fair" that my father died at sixty-nine?

Many people die at much younger ages.

Is it "fair" that my father, and I, lived at all?

When it comes to lifespan, what claims of fairness can be made? The fact that we are alive contains an element of mystery that is impenetrable.

Life often unfolds in ways that are at odds with our ideas of fairness. Our ideas of fairness can be beautiful and there is nothing wrong with holding onto them. However, if our attachment to those ideas causes us to resist reality we add to our suffering.

My father's death caused me great sadness. My efforts to keep my old story alive caused additional suffering.

It takes time to relinquish the stories we love and replace them with truth. And the more time it takes, the more we will suffer.

This doesn't mean we should short-circuit the grieving process and attempt to jump straight to equanimity.

However, a deep love of truth and of what is, was, and will be (YHWH) helps us move through grief.

Our perpetual dissatisfaction takes many forms.

"I want my parent/spouse/sibling/friend to treat me the way I want to be treated!" "I want the world to more closely resemble how I imagine the world should be!"

But your parent/spouse/sibling/friend treats you the way they treat you. And the world is as it is, not as you imagine it to be.

This doesn't mean that we should stop trying to improve our relationships or give up on advancing our highest ideals. It means that our efforts for improvement should start from recognizing what is.

In spiritual circles, this is sometimes expressed as "letting go." We let go of our ideas about how things should be and accept the reality of how things actually are.

Many people fight this idea. We know from our personal histories that it can take great effort to improve upon difficult situations. That effort may feel like the very opposite of letting go and accepting. Letting go and accepting can be interpreted as giving up.

Giving up is not what I am suggesting.

"Accepting what is" means that if you are in a bad situation, you should acknowledge exactly how bad it is. This very acknowledgment may help provide the energy required to make change. It may also help you realize the depth of change that is necessary.

Even if you are unable to change a bad situation, acknowledging what is can lead you to take the wisest actions that are available.

Reality is often difficult and brutal. And the stories we tell ourselves are powerful and can be hard to abandon, even if they no longer serve us well.

Loving truth, loving reality, isn't always easy. But the alternative is to fight against life itself. And if you fight against life itself, you will lose.

When you love what is true, you won't escape sadness. Instead, sadness will become one experience within the totality of experiences.

Truth is all-inclusive. Sadness exists, but so does happiness. Both are temporary states that will arise and pass away.

When we experience sadness, we want the feeling to go away. And when we experience happiness, we want the feeling to remain.

When the impulse to hold on to happiness arises, the desire not to lose happiness replaces the experience of happiness. And when we try to push sadness away, sadness remains and may even deepen.

The psychologist Carl Jung observed that "what you resist not only persists but grows in size."

Push away, hold on. Push away, hold on. This is the work of ego. It is the energy we expend to keep ourselves perpetually dissatisfied.

A question we constantly ask ourselves, even if we don't realize it, is "How can I feel better?" This is the voice of ego.

Without dissatisfaction, ego is lost. It is the nature of ego to want.

Most of spiritual life, as well as the rest of our lives, is motivated by this desire to feel better.

When we dislike how we feel, if we are upset, sad, or dissatisfied, we will do almost anything to shift our negative experience.

Even when we feel good, we will chase something that promises to make us feel better. Ego wants to want even more than ego wants to have.

If I eat, will I feel better? Will watching TV or looking at my phone help me feel better? Will prayer, meditation, learning, reading, exercising, a new relationship, etc., help me to feel better?

Even if this question isn't at the top of our mind, it's always close by, exerting its influence upon us.

To remain in charge of our lives, ego needs to keep us dissatisfied, in a state of wanting. Most people live the entirety of their lives as slaves to perpetual wanting.

The desire to have more, even when we have enough, comes from ego. The desire to have a spouse or partner who fits our image of perfection comes from ego. And the desire to be close to God in order to feel better comes from ego.

Our nonstop preoccupation with feeling better makes it difficult for us to sit with the following question:

If I stopped trying to feel better, would I feel better?

And this raises other questions:

Am I capable of stopping myself from trying to feel better? Can I accept everything as it is, completely and totally, with no fights, arguments, or disagreements? Even if only for a short time?

What would happen if ego sometimes ceased to be in control? Sometimes we wouldn't experience dissatisfaction.

What would happen if ego ceased to be in control most of the time? Most of the time, we wouldn't experience dissatisfaction.

What would happen if ego was never in control? We would never experience dissatisfaction.[3]

Dissatisfaction is different from sadness and suffering. No matter where you are on your spiritual journey, you may still have occasion to be sad and to suffer. But ideally, the sadness and suffering will move through you. You won't try to escape sadness by chasing the idea that if only the world conformed to your preferences your sadness would disappear. Instead, sadness and suffering will arise and fall away, along with a myriad of other insights, emotions, and experiences.

Reality is in constant motion. Accepting everything as it is means embracing constant change.

The "you" that is the nothing that is everything doesn't have an incessant desire for more. Its nature is to be satisfied with what is.

The nature of the nothing that is everything is also love. When I use the word *love*, I mean the deep connection that binds us all together. Like the word *God*, the word *love* has been used to mean so many different things that it is easily misunderstood. And as with the word *God*, the word *love* is useful only if it helps you recognize what you experience. If love becomes an ideal to chase, then ego is in control.

The experience of love is compassion extended broadly. When we are in touch with love, there is a natural desire to ease suffering. Broad and deep compassion creates a call to action. Discerning how to respond wisely to the world's suffering is part of the journey.

It is possible for the nothing that is everything to love life exactly as it is and at the same time desire to ease suffering. It is a paradox that must be experienced rather than explained.

Repairing the World

The idea of "repairing the world" comes from the mystical side of Jewish tradition. The mystics' creation story posits that the world we live in is not (yet) the world that was originally planned. According to this story, the process of creating the world caused sparks of divinity to be inadvertently scattered everywhere. The world's problems arise because these sparks aren't yet in their proper locations.

In the mystics' version of creation, humans become cocreators. Our task is to gather the scattered sparks of divinity and restore them to their originally planned locations. This restoration project is the "repair" the mystical tradition tells us needs to occur.

The mystics' creation narrative provides a clever explanation for how a perfect deity could create a seemingly imperfect world. The creation isn't yet complete. The imperfection we see provides humans with the ability to become God's partners in creating the world.

For the Jewish mystics, repairing the world begins by seeing the divine in everything. Only when divinity is recognized can it be restored to its proper place.

On a practical level, this can be understood as seeing the potential for good (the divine spark) even if that potential has not yet been actualized.

A story in the Talmud relates that Rabbi Meir was harassed by some neighborhood gangsters. His wife, Bruriah, overheard him praying that they should die. Bruriah chastised Meir, telling him that instead of praying for their death, he should pray for their transformation. Meir followed Bruriah's advice, and the neighborhood gangsters changed their ways.[4]

At first, Meir saw only the flaws. Bruriah helped him see the potential for good that was hidden by those flaws.

The conventional idea of "repair" contains the assumption that something is broken. Contemporary approaches to "repairing the world" often emphasize problems. It is common to hear that the world needs repair, not because there is divinity everywhere that needs love and attention, but because the world is filled with injustice.

I don't recommend hiding from the realities of injustice. But when motivations to do good are rooted in seeing division, there is a likelihood that division will be reinforced. Ego tells you that your vision of the world is a better vision than someone else's. If you win, they lose, and vice versa. When ego sees pain and injustice it often responds with an anger that can reinforce separation.

The nothing that is everything sees the pain and injustice and responds with love.

This response is as natural as making sure a child doesn't touch a hot stove. Until the child understands the dangers, precautionary actions will be necessary. The desire of the child to touch the stove creates conflict. The conflict is real, as is the potential harm. But the conflict is managed through love rather than division.

You can bring this same intention to conflicts with close friends or family members. If division predominates, working through the conflict becomes about winning and losing. No matter who wins, the relationship is likely to be damaged. When love predominates, working through the conflict demonstrates that you value the relationship. Valuing the relationship doesn't require that you give up on what's important to you. But it does require a recognition that there's more at stake than simply getting your way.

When we respond with love, we naturally want to ameliorate suffering. Love doesn't try to "win."

A person who is suffering probably doesn't care whether

the help they receive is motivated by seeing divisions or by love (the correlate of seeing divinity everywhere). I certainly don't want to talk anyone out of performing good deeds, even if those good deeds are motivated by ego. But to the extent that we remain locked in a view that sees only division, we are likely to perpetuate suffering. Even the best of intentions can't protect us from ego's negative effects.

For example, without armed resistance, I am certain Nazi Germany's genocidal impulses and desires for world conquest would have created even greater suffering. By becoming involved in World War II, the United States helped end Hitler's reign of terror. But during the war, the United States placed Japanese Americans in internment camps. This is widely seen as one of the worst civil rights violations in American history. The drumbeats of war that led the United States to oppose Nazi Germany also led to the Japanese internment camps.

It's possible to imagine the United States actively opposing Nazi Germany without placing Japanese Americans in internment camps. But the U.S. population and administration would have needed to see the world differently to have avoided that civil rights disaster.

One way to repair the world is to work on repairing ourselves.

The Ethics of Unity

A human being is a part of the whole, called by us "Universe," a part limited in time and space. He

> *experiences himself, his thoughts and feelings as*
> *something separated from the rest—a kind of optical*
> *delusion of his consciousness. This delusion is a kind of*
> *prison for us, restricting us to our personal desires and*
> *to affection for a few persons nearest to us. Our task*
> *must be to free ourselves from this prison by widening*
> *our circle of compassion to embrace all living creatures*
> *and the whole of nature in its beauty. —Albert Einstein*

When I realized that I was what I was seeking, something inside of me relaxed. I experienced a welcome sense of contentment and ease. Although this was extremely pleasant, there were ways in which it was also unsettling.

For years, ego's dissatisfaction and desire for more kept me very busy. When ego was no longer in charge, ego's motivations fell away. And without these motivations, I no longer knew what I should be doing.

Some people may find that ego's drives are immediately replaced by the wisdom of conscious awareness. But this was not my experience. It has taken me years to adjust to my new reality. For a long time, I wondered whether I would ever again feel a sense of motivation.

Over time, new motivations have taken shape. For example, I have a sense that it's my role to write this book. In the past, the reason to write would be to serve another goal. I might have written with a vision of large-scale impact. My grand visions provided me with a great deal of energy.

Now my motivations are less grand. It's not entirely clear to me why I'm writing. But I find myself sitting at a computer and working to communicate as clearly as I can. I don't know what comes next, nor do I need to know.

Many religious texts promise prosperity and good fortune for the pious. Yet, a passage in the Talmud tells us that proper actions should be done "for their own sake."[5] The passage tells us that the promises of good fortune are a way to get people in the door. At first, people will act because they are promised a reward. But eventually, and ideally, the behaviors may come to be done "for their own sake."

I laugh at myself when my old, egoic motivations attempt to take hold. The voice of ego is still there, but I can no longer take it seriously—at least not for very long.

The motivations of conscious awareness are still growing within me. I am learning to live with a different sense of agency. I can't predict where this will lead. Nor do I try to predict. Instead, I allow life to take shape within me and through me. In reality, life takes shape within me and through me regardless of whether I allow it. But allowing it provides a different experience.

I don't have a "purpose" that I'm trying to fulfill. I still have occasion to think strategically and execute plans that have future implications. But I am motivated by the "next right action" rather than a vision of the future.

If acting ethically and compassionately has been motivated by ego, removing this motivation appears dangerous. The fear that the world will fall apart without ego's motivations is a trick ego plays to maintain its hold on us.

When ego moves from the proverbial driver's seat to the passenger's seat, it may take a while before you get used to the new driver. And conscious awareness may drive you to different locations than ego used to. But the vehicle keeps moving.

Still, a question remains. If the world is as it should be, why would anyone act ethically?

Ethical and compassionate actions arise naturally from unity consciousness.

The biblical verse "love your neighbor as yourself," has served as a foundation for ethical teachings. From separation consciousness, this verse teaches that people should place themselves in the shoes of their neighbor and behave accordingly. This is an important mental exercise for those living within separation consciousness.

Unity consciousness offers a different view. It understands this verse to mean that your neighbor is a part of you. And you are a part of your neighbor.[6] You and your neighbor belong to a single organism.

When living within unity consciousness, you don't need to imagine what it's like to be in your neighbor's shoes. The view from unity consciousness is that you *are* your neighbor.

This is how the Sufi teacher Inayat Khan expressed this idea:

> *Humanity is as one single body, and all nations*
> *and communities and races as the different organs,*
> *and the happiness and well-being of each of them*
> *is the happiness and well-being of the whole body.*

If there is one organ of the body in pain, the whole
body has to sustain a share of the strain of it.[7]

This understanding helps us to imagine the behaviors that might arise from an ethic of unity.

If my left hand receives a wound, I won't hesitate to take care of it. And if the wound becomes infected, I will take action to ensure that the infection doesn't spread to the rest of my body. The recognition that your neighbor is a part of you leads to responding to their wounds in the same way. With this recognition, empathy, care, and wise boundaries arise naturally.

The lived experience of unity gives rise to its own set of behaviors. This goes beyond adopting unity as an idea, and then extrapolating behaviors from this idea. That approach might yield many good results. But *imagining* unity is different from *experiencing* unity.

In imagined unity, an individual's behaviors can arise from the mind attempting to impose its will. This approach will often lead to wise behaviors. But the approach will break down when the mind's abilities fall short, and it is unable to control behaviors through ideas alone. Human beings are complicated, and while ideas matter, ego's endless quest to "make me feel better" remains a powerful force. Still, absent the experience of unity, it's wise to substitute the ethics of imagined unity.

From within the experience of unity, it is rarely necessary to figure out how best to behave. The behaviors arise naturally and are rooted in love.

Living in a State of Flow

If you have ever "lost yourself" within an activity, you probably weren't trying to hold on to the experience, nor were you trying to push it away. There was nothing to push away, and nothing to hold on to. Instead, you were immersed in whatever it was you were doing.

There is a natural joy that arises when we are in this state of flow.

Losing yourself in a state of flow is different from losing yourself while watching a mediocre TV show or after drinking enough alcohol. Losing yourself in alcohol and TV are typically attempts to make yourself feel better. In these instances, consciousness becomes muted rather than enhanced.

Ego tries to convince us that if it were to be replaced by unity consciousness, we would behave unethically, lose all motivation, and take no actions. But this isn't correct. Instead of ego's drive to "make me feel better," unity consciousness has its own, unpredictable way of operating.

During the heightened consciousness experience of a state of flow, you aren't attempting to make yourself feel better. You are just being. It may feel as if life is taking shape through you rather than attempting to mold life to conform to your ideas. In these moments of flow, our constructed self recedes. When we talk about "losing ourselves" in an activity, the self that is lost is our constructed identity.

All that has to happen to regularly experience the joy of those moments is to stop holding on and pushing away.

It sounds as if it should be easy, and in a sense, it is. It takes much more energy to keep pushing away and holding on than to stop pushing away and holding on.

Once we recognize we are in a state of flow, however, it usually ends. Ego notices that the flow state feels good and wants to hold on to it. The effort to hold on is incompatible with the experience of flow.

If you have experienced a state of flow, you may have noticed this dynamic. You may have been immersed in a game, work, gardening, appreciating nature, or in some other activity. Then, you took a moment to reflect on the fact that you were experiencing a sense of ease, joy, and contentment and tried to hold on to it, after which it became difficult to recapture the same natural ease that was present only moments before.

It is one thing to briefly experience awakened consciousness. It is another thing to sustain and live within awakened consciousness.

When I live from awakened consciousness, I'm not trying to feel better. And ironically, when I stop trying to feel better, it feels better.

For awakened consciousness to become the place from which you live, you need to stop holding on and pushing away. This often requires practice.

> When I stop trying to feel better, it feels better.

In the next chapter, we will explore religious and spiritual practices. At their best, these practices are tools that can help us live from awakened consciousness. And these same practices can, at their worst, reinforce the impulse to hold on and push away.

KEY TAKEAWAYS

- Having an experience of conscious awareness is not the same as living from conscious awareness. Living from conscious awareness may take some practice.
- Ego keeps us dissatisfied by pushing away and holding on.
- When we stop pushing away and holding on, we enter a state of flow.
- The nature of the nothing that is everything is to accept what is.
- To accept what is does not preclude changing it.
- The nature of the nothing that is everything is love.

Chapter 6

Religious and Spiritual Practices

Toward the end of the eighteenth century, a disciple traveled to the town of Mezritch to study with the renowned preacher of the town. After several years of study, he decided he was ready to return home. On the way, he stopped in the town of Karlin to visit Rabbi Aaron, who for a time had been his study partner in the great preacher's school.

It was nearly midnight when the disciple reached the city, but his desire to see his friend was so great that he went to his house. He saw light coming from a window and knocked on the door. He heard the familiar voice ask, "Who is it?" Certain that his own voice would be recognized he answered: "I!" But the door remained closed. No other sound came from within, though he knocked again and again.

At last, he called out in distress: "Aaron, why don't you open for me?" Aaron replied, in a voice so solemn that it sounded almost strange to him: "Who is it that dares call himself 'I' as befits only God!" When the disciple heard this, he said to himself: "I have not learned nearly enough," and without delaying he returned to Mezritch.

Ego Is Left Behind

In this story, Aaron teaches a lesson to his friend. Yet Aaron appears contracted and unkind whereas his friend is filled with an openhearted affection. Perhaps Aaron's teaching style fit the situation perfectly. But perhaps it was unnecessarily harsh. Only Aaron and his friend can know. And even they are likely to become confused.

Just as ego wants to swim underwater and fly, it may also want to achieve spiritual heights. The experience of unity consciousness can provide ego with more identity content. Ego may use the experience of unity to appear as a spiritually developed being. Or in its constant quest to feel better, ego may chase the rewards of happiness and fulfillment that spirituality promises. Yet, when oneness is fully recognized, the process of identity construction is left behind. The process still exists, but it has become a humorous sideshow instead of the main event. If unity consciousness becomes your lived reality, it may be disconcerting to ego.

Egoic consciousness can lead us toward unity consciousness. But when unity consciousness breaks through, egoic consciousness isn't there to enjoy it.

With a recognition of oneness, the egoic "I" hasn't achieved anything. The egoic "I" hasn't become aware of anything.

"I" am not aware. Awareness is aware. The egoic "I" that awareness now perceives is seen for what it has always been: a collection of sometimes deep, often petty, but always ephemeral, thoughts.

The first word of the Ten Commandments, and according to one interpretation the only word that God actually spoke to the people gathered at Mt. Sinai, is "I."[1]

From the perspective of unity consciousness, there is only one true identity, only one "I."

> *"Who is it that dares call himself 'I' as befits only God!" When the disciple heard this, he said to himself: "I have not learned nearly enough," and without delaying he returned to Mezritch.*

Stories, Beliefs, and Behaviors

It is powerful to recognize that there is only one true "I" in the universe. Yet it's practical and helpful to use the word *I* when referring to yourself. We are all part of the universal "I," with our unique backgrounds, personalities, and experiences.

If we're lucky, somewhere along the way we realize our identity as part of the universal "I." Typically, this realization occurs after immersion within a religious or spiritual tradition.

What is realized is universal. But spiritual paths are particular.

Spiritual and religious traditions provide stories, beliefs, and behaviors designed to bring us to the recognition of who we truly are. The stories are compiled in books like the Koran, Mahabharata, and the Bible. The beliefs are transmitted through written and oral traditions. And the behaviors include prayer, meditation, chant, study, practices surrounding the activities of daily life, and more. Religious and spiritual traditions create a path for their adherents. These paths are designed to bring people to a recognition of what is, a recognition of unity.

Science is another path to recognizing what is. Unlike the religious traditions, science did not begin with an experience of unity. Modern science has nevertheless led to the discovery of a deep unity that lies underneath, and within, the observed diversity of the world.

None of these paths are flawless. And it is possible to learn from each of them. There are scientists who align themselves with a religious tradition, and it is not unusual for atheists to meditate.

Supporters of each path can boast of achievements and lament failures. I am not defending or promoting any of these paths. The motivations, purposes, and outcomes of these paths already fill many books. My purpose here is to bring attention to something they have in common. All these paths want to help people see the world as it truly is.

We humans are social creatures. If we have insights into how the world operates, we want to share those insights with others. To share insights with others, scientists rely on replicating experimental results. If the results of an experiment can't be replicated, the experiment is of no value.

For centuries, religions have wrestled with the challenge of how to share spiritual insights. This challenge has produced masterpieces of storytelling and literature. And it has produced suggested, or mandated, beliefs and behaviors.

Ideally, these stories, beliefs, and behaviors lead to experiences of unity consciousness. The stories, beliefs, and behaviors also provide guidance for how to live when we are stuck within egoic consciousness.

Religious teachings attempt to transmit the value of spiritual experiences to others. But spiritual experiences aren't easily captured in stories, beliefs, and behaviors. These experiences penetrate to a place beyond language, beyond beliefs, and beyond behavior. Something is bound to get lost in transmission.

Any and all attempts to convey spiritual experiences will fall short. By definition, these experiences exceed language's ability to capture them. This is not a condemnation of religious practices and teachings. It is a reminder that even as these practices and teachings are meant to be helpful, they can also cause confusion and lead us astray.

Today, we would be shocked to hear that Vatican authorities kidnapped a six-year-old Jewish child so he would be raised as a Catholic. But this is exactly what happened to Edgardo Mortara in 1858 in Bologna, Italy. The child had been ill and was secretly baptized by a Catholic worker in the Mortara household. The worker was afraid Edgardo would go to hell if he died unbaptized. Her actions may have been wrong, but her motives were benign. The Vatican laws that governed Bologna at that time didn't allow a Catholic child to be raised by Jews. The Vatican, under orders from Pope Pius IX, kidnapped Edgardo and raised him in a home for Catholic converts. I am quite certain Pope Pius IX acted in what he believed were the child's best interests.

There are many such examples. In an effort to bring redemption to the world, the Jewish Frankist movement (named for its founder, Jacob Frank, 1726–1791) encouraged breaking every rule and transgressing every boundary. Sunni and Shiite Muslims have a long history of sectarian violence. Buddhist monks have led the persecution of a Moslem minority in Burma. And the Hindu caste system has perpetuated generations of suffering.

The originators of Catholicism, Judaism, Islam, Buddhism, and Hinduism didn't intend for their teachings to lead to greater suffering. Whether religious teachings and practices are helpful or harmful is in the hands of the individuals who engage with them.

The history of science tells us that it too can, and most likely will, be used in both helpful and harmful ways.

Harmful scientific experiments have been conducted on people without their knowledge or consent. Technology has amplified our power to destroy. And the scale of environmental degradation that we have seen in the 21st century would have been impossible without the contributions of science.

Misuse and abuse take place on a grand scale. They also take place within individuals.

People usually aren't pleased to hear that their beloved tradition or practice carries the potential of personal harm. It is more comfortable to think that the performance of religious practices guarantees benefit. Unfortunately, that's not the case.

> *A joke is told of three people in synagogue on Yom Kippur, the holiest day of the Jewish year, praying with the congregation for forgiveness. One of them is praying with particular fervor. He loudly laments his poor behavior from the past year and pleads with God for forgiveness, even though he is unworthy.*
>
> *The two other people overhear his prayers and notice his fervor. One says to the other:*
> *"Look who thinks he's nothing."*

The joke "works" on a few different levels. The two people passing negative judgment on the prayers of their neighbor, is an all too human scene. And indeed, the person praying with fervor might be performing piety rather than inhabiting it. Even humility can be cultivated to serve our arrogance.

The process of identity construction is extraordinarily clever and relentless. It can use anything, including prayer and meditation, for its own purposes.

Religions and Schools of Thought

There are many schools of thought (e.g., philosophy and science). And there are many spiritual paths. If you identify with a school of thought or spiritual path, it may help diminish the grip of ego. But there is no way to guarantee permanent sanctuary from the process of identity construction.

If identification with a particular path helps you diminish the grip of ego, it carries the seeds of its own undoing. As ego unravels, all identities that fortify it are seen more clearly. I used to identify with my body, thoughts, emotions, with Judaism, and with many other aspects of myself. Although I no longer identify with them, I still have a body, thoughts, and emotions. And I still have Judaism.

Apparently, I needed to go through a period of identification before I could begin the process of disidentifying. Disidentifying doesn't mean disavowing or renouncing. It means coming to know the various aspects of yourself and relating to them wisely. Identification gives way to disidentification, which can lead us to wisdom. As we saw in chapter four, your body, thoughts, and emotions can serve as gateways to helping you understand who you are. Used wisely, religions and schools of thought can also serve as gateways.

We all have both constructed and unconstructed identities. Remember, ego has a role to play. But unacknowledged ego will block out the experience of conscious awareness.

Every school of thought and every spiritual path can, and most likely will, cause harm.

I have gained a great deal from practicing yoga. And I have injured myself practicing yoga. I have seen how being part of a religious community can be beautifully supportive. And I have seen how being part of a religious community can create hostility.

Don't discard a school of thought or spiritual path because it can, and most likely will, lead to some negative effects. Instead, to the greatest extent possible, exercise wisdom. Stay connected to the truth to which your path points, rather than giving full fidelity to protecting its forms.

The spiritual teacher Adyashanti, who immersed himself for many years in Zen Buddhism, said that "The goal of Buddhism is to create Buddhas, not Buddhists. The goal of Christianity is to create Christs, not Christians."

This same sentiment can be applied to other religious paths as well. The goal is not to perpetuate fidelity to the forms and institutions. The goal is transformation.

Perhaps one day the current articulation of ideas within your chosen path will join the fate of all other ideas and recede into the background. The forms (rituals, institutions, etc.) too are destined to change and eventually give way to other forms. Today's oldest paths and schools of thought trace their lineage back four thousand years. Humans have been around for three hundred thousand years, and earth is 4.5 billion years old. Nothing lasts forever.

It is possible, though unusual, for awakening to occur without immersion in an established tradition. But simply waiting for spiritual lightning to strike is unlikely to be effective.

Still, there is no absolute need to attach yourself to a school of thought or spiritual path. And it certainly isn't necessary to abandon a school of thought or spiritual path.

The issue is not whether you choose to follow or leave a spiritual path. The issue is whether you have formed an entrenched identity around these choices.

In the story with which we began this chapter, the disciple chose to return to the great preacher of Mezritch to continue his learning. But his years of study in Mezritch hadn't produced the results he was looking for. Perhaps he would have been better off staying in Karlin to learn from his friend Aaron.

On the other hand, Aaron had gained his learning in Mezritch. And Aaron's response to his friend was harsh. Did Aaron really need to keep his friend waiting outside after a long journey? Was this the right moment, and the right way, for Aaron to teach that the only true "I" in the universe is God? Perhaps returning to Mezritch was indeed the better choice for the disciple.

If you were the disciple, what would you have done? Continue with the teacher with whom you started, or change teachers?

You are free to determine your relationship to established schools of thought and spiritual paths.

Metaphor Management

"Relationship with God" is a common metaphor designed to be helpful. But it may lead to confusion.

If God, spirit, conscious awareness (pick whichever words you prefer) is what you *are*, what is meant by "relationship?"

Egoic consciousness imagines that pure being will be found by looking within or beyond oneself. According to the relationship metaphor, once pure being is found, we can "relate" to it. When egoic consciousness is occupying center stage, this metaphor may "work" as it speaks to ego's perceptions. But pure being is what you are, not something you perceive to exist only within or beyond you. From within unity consciousness, the relationship metaphor breaks down.

Typically, egoic consciousness will have its day before unity consciousness is realized. The relationship metaphor speaks ego's language and when ego is in charge, ego needs to be addressed. We may need to become somebody before we can awaken to the nothing that is everything.

But the metaphor of relationship may hold us back by reinforcing the idea that egoic consciousness will stay in charge. "'I' have a relationship with God" says much more about "I" than it does about God.

The relationship metaphor carries the danger of strengthening egoic consciousness. Ego will fool you into thinking it is doing exactly the opposite.

Joke: What did the spiritual seeker say to the hot dog seller?

"Make me one with everything!"

Spiritual paths will sometimes state the goal of spiritual life as "becoming one with everything." But, like the relationship metaphor, this metaphor may also lead us astray.

Seeking or achieving oneness implies it isn't already present. You can't "*become* one with everything" if you already *are* one with everything.

The implication of "*becoming* one with everything" is that there is something you can do to change the state of the universe from divided to unified.

Worse, it implies that only *you* become one with everything, while the rest of the world remains in its divided state.

When we discover who we really are, we also recognize that this is what we have always been. Who we are was never beyond us. Who we are, by definition, *can't* be beyond us.

We can't become one with everything. Everything is already one.

Becoming one, and cultivating a relationship, are metaphors. They attempt to make sense of the spiritual journey from within egoic consciousness. They also have the effect of reinforcing egoic consciousness.

Ego is very cunning.

Knowing that these metaphors are speaking on ego's terms may help you use them to loosen ego's grip rather than reinforce it. Alternatively, once the distortions contained within these metaphors are recognized, you might choose to abandon them, at least for a time. Open up to the possibility that you don't need to develop a relationship with God, nor do you need to become one with anything. Nothing needs to change.

All that needs to happen is that you stop fooling yourself and recognize WhoWhatWhere you really are.

The Purpose of Spiritual Practice

In an effort to move beyond ego, religious and spiritual practices will often speak to ego in its own language. The wise practitioner must learn when ego is being reinforced and when it is being weakened.

Religious and spiritual practices have many purposes. They perpetuate established institutions. They create group identities that lead to a sense of belonging. And they have the potential to bring positive psychological and social benefit. But their most important purpose is to help us see ourselves and the world as we truly are.

One strategy employed by religious and spiritual practices to help us see ourselves as we are is to exhaust the process of identity construction. It takes a lot of energy to keep us from recognizing our unconstructed identities. If we stopped exerting this energy, we would immediately recognize WhoWhatWhere we really are.

Many people will argue with this insight. It seems as if it takes no energy for the process of identity construction to keep humming along and that it takes effort to allow the experience of our unconstructed identities to break through. And even if you do manage to realize unity, the realization is usually temporary. It soon falls away and is replaced by the perception of division. This may lead you to conclude that perceiving division is easy, whereas realizing unity is hard.

In reality, it takes a lot of work to feed ego's needs.

In its attempts to stay in charge, ego determines that it can perceive unity if it just tries hard enough. Exerting energy to perceive unity is ego hard at work. "*I want to perceive unity!*" is the voice of the process of identity construction. And as long as this voice is prominent, we will be stuck within division.

It's a vicious circle. The motivation for spiritual growth gets caught within the process of identity construction. If we don't find a way to break this circle, we will never get beyond it.

In steps religious practice. It keeps the process of identity construction safely occupied with a great deal of activity so it can eventually wear itself out. Regular prayer, meditation, and rituals, if we are diligent and lucky, engage and eventually exhaust ego. When ego is too exhausted to maintain its grip, it lets go, even if just for a moment.

When ego lets go, you lose your (egoic) self. When you lose yourself, you enter a state of flow.

Letting go of the process of identity construction allows our true identities to shine through.

Letting Go

Imagine a person holding a ball in one hand. The person has been holding this ball for years. The arm and hand muscles have become very strong, but those same muscles are getting tired. It is difficult for the person to accomplish certain tasks, given that one hand is always occupied.

The person wants to let go of the ball but doesn't know how. Many people offer advice.

"Just let go!" they say.

"But how do I let go?"

"Relax your arm and hand."

"But how do I relax my arm and hand?"

And so it goes until one day a different strategy is suggested.

"Hold on tighter! Squeeze that ball with everything you've got!"

Following this advice, perhaps for moments, perhaps for days or even years, the muscles exhaust themselves and the ball is finally released.[2]

Hold tight to let go. This is the path of spiritual practices.

Alternatively, you can just let go.

Some people come to the awakened state without the aid of any practice. Somehow, they figure out how to let go. But it seems to be more common for spiritual realization to come after engaging with spiritual practices.

> Hold tight to let go. This is the path of spiritual practices.

As you engage with spiritual practices, be aware of ego's relentless efforts to co-opt those practices for additional identity construction. As Ramana Maharshi said: "The question 'Who am I?' is not really meant to get an answer. The question 'Who am I?' is meant to dissolve the questioner."

Spiritual techniques and traditions can help you exhaust the process of identity construction. Knowing this may help you on your journey.

Holding On

All techniques and traditions can be helpful or harmful depending upon the spirit in which they are practiced. It is easy to become competitive, with oneself or with others. This desire to outdo can sometimes help spur us along. But this desire arises from the process of identity construction. If that fact goes unacknowledged, then competition and comparison become a trap that holds us back.

There is a Jewish custom of reciting at least one hundred blessings a day. When the blessings recited during prayers and meals are counted, reaching one hundred blessings a day is quite realistic. The purpose of all these blessings is to foster an attitude of gratitude, appreciation, and wonder.

Once, when leaving a Jewish community meeting in the late afternoon, the few participants walked outside and observed a beautiful rainbow. They stopped to take in the sight, appreciating the magical colors in the sky.

"Amazing."

"Beautiful."

Then someone asked, "What's the blessing you're supposed to recite when seeing a rainbow?"[3]

"I think it's about the biblical story of Noah," one person replied.

"No, I don't think that's it. But I can't remember what it is."

Knowledge is typically prized within the Jewish community. The person who could come up with the answer would immediately gain status. And there is tacit communal agreement that everyone should want to acquire more learning.

One person went to their phone to look up the blessing.

The others waited for the answer. By the time the answer was found, the rainbow had disappeared.

The tradition of blessings had caused the small gathering to become distracted. In this case, the custom of reciting blessings had interrupted their sense of wonder and appreciation.

Reciting blessings, becoming educated and knowledgeable, sitting for hours in meditation, being pious and devout—they can all work for us, or against us. When they help us let go, they are working for us. When they reinforce ego, they are working against us.

Ego will do whatever it can to maintain its place.

None of this has value if it is accepted as an idea. It only has value if it is experienced.

Practices that disrupt the process of identity construction help you along your journey. But if these practices become tools of ego, they should be reevaluated. The practices can be discarded or rebooted, but they shouldn't be allowed to remain as ego's servants.

"My tradition is better than anyone else's tradition."

"I'm an excellent meditator."

"I'm a good Christian/Jew/Muslim/Buddhist, etc."

Thoughts such as these are signals that your practices may be serving ego.

Even the thought, "Engaging in these practices gives my life meaning," is a sign that the process of identity construction is hard at work.

Your true nature doesn't "find" meaning, nor does it need to. Finding is the result of seeking. Ego's nature is to be unsatisfied and to seek.

The meaning of your existence is unquestioned and self-evident when *your* existence and existence itself are one and the same.

Religious traditions and spiritual practices should help bring us to this self-evident place.

Unfortunately, it is often the case that spiritual practices, and science as well, become ways for us to reinforce ego's sovereignty. Their true purpose is to move ego to its rightful place as court jester—occasionally entertaining, cleverly prodding us forward, but never in charge.

How you practice is much more important than what you practice. Deep inquiry conducted with unflinching honesty can help keep you on track.

Spiritual practices should exhaust the seeker and dethrone the process of identity construction. They should bring you to the recognition that conscious awareness, the nothing that is everything, is WhoWhatWhere you are.

Speaking Ego's Language

The quiet awareness that has always been present doesn't insist that you know of its existence. But if unity consciousness manages to break through, ego's approach to life can appear silly. Ego has its role to play. But living an entire lifetime from within ego's limited perspective is an odd existence.

Rabbi Nahman from the town of Bratzlav (1772–1810) told this story:

Once upon a time, a prince decided he was a turkey.

He sat naked under the table, pecking at bones and pieces of bread, just like a turkey. The royal physicians spoke to him, begging him to come out from under the table and behave like a prince. After years of trying, they gave up hope of curing him. The king and queen grieved tremendously.

A sage arrived and said, "I will cure him."

The sage undressed and sat naked under the table, next to the prince, picking crumbs and bones. "Who are you?" asked the prince. "What are you doing here?"

"And you?" replied the sage. "What are you doing here?"

"I am a turkey," said the prince. "I'm also a turkey," answered the sage.

They sat together like this for some time, until they became good friends. One day, the sage requested to receive two shirts. He said to the prince, "What makes you think that a turkey can't wear a shirt? You can wear a shirt and still be a turkey." With that, the two of them put on shirts.

After a while, the sage requested two pairs of pants. As before, he asked, "What makes you think you can't be a turkey if you wear pants?"

The sage continued in this manner until they were both completely dressed. Then he asked for regular food, from the table. The sage said, "What makes you think that you will stop being a turkey if you eat good food? You can eat whatever you want and still be a turkey!" They both ate the food.

Finally, the sage said, "What makes you think a turkey must sit under the table? Even a turkey can sit at the table."

The sage continued in this manner until one day the prince awoke and realized he wasn't a turkey.

In theory, the prince could have woken up at any moment and realized he wasn't a turkey. But the illusion of turkey consciousness is hard to recognize when you think you are a turkey.

We too can wake up at any moment.

Ideally, religious and spiritual teachings and practices serve the role of the sage in the story. They speak to ego in terms it can understand and skillfully bring us to the awakened state.

KEY TAKEAWAYS

+ Religious and spiritual practices speak to ego on its own terms.
+ Practices can exhaust ego, but they also carry the danger of reinforcing and strengthening ego.
+ Ego stays active and keeps us dissatisfied by pushing away and holding on. We can stop pushing away and holding on at any time. We just need to let go.
+ When ego stops exerting the energy to hold on and push away, you become aware of the awareness that is and has always been, WhoWhatWhere you are.

Chapter 7

Freedom and Belonging

I long, as does every human being, to be at home wherever I find myself.

—Maya Angelou

WE ALL WANT TO BE free, yet the meaning and experience of freedom are elusive.

We hold beliefs about freedom, but often we do not closely examine them. Some of these beliefs may be inhibiting freedom.

What are your beliefs about freedom?

The Passover seder is an annual exploration of freedom. Each year, as part of the seder ritual, Jews recite "This year we are slaves; next year we shall be free." There is irony in knowing that when we return to the ritual the following year, we will recite these same words again. Personally, I am not satisfied by the notion that freedom is something I will always pursue but never experience.

Freedom

A common understanding of freedom is being able to do what I want when I want. At first, it sounds appealing. But we would be very concerned if tomorrow were proclaimed Freedom Day and the whole world was expected to act out this understanding of freedom.

An ancient teaching tells us that we only truly possess what we give away.[1] What is the freedom you can grant to others that you also wish to have for yourself?

You can grant everyone the freedom to be exactly as they are.

This doesn't mean that you agree with everyone's opinions or approve of all their choices. It means you stop insisting that the world conform to your version of how things should be. Instead, you accept that things are as they are.

When you allow everyone the freedom to be exactly as they are, you also give this gift to yourself. You are included in "everyone." This means you give up the belief that others should agree with, approve of, or understand you. Holding this belief inhibits your freedom. You get to be exactly as you are, with all your flaws, beauty, uniqueness, and individuality.

Individuation

The word *individual* contains an interesting truth. Individual means "not divided." To be an individual means to be undivided within yourself and undivided from everything else.

Becoming an individual is a process. The psychologist Carl Jung called this maturation process "individuation."

Individuation takes place both internally and externally. Internally, we combine and integrate all aspects of ourselves into a coherent whole. Externally, we come to understand that our seemingly separate lives are intimately connected to all of life. As we mature, we develop both the internal and external aspects of this process.

We tend to think that an individual is someone who "goes their own way" and "stands apart from the crowd." And there is partial truth to that understanding. But a true individual must simultaneously "stand apart from" and "stand together with." To be a true individual means to be undivided.

When we "stand apart from," we experience our unique-ness and our freedom. When we "stand together with," we experience our commonality and our belonging. We are one, yet we are autonomous; we belong, yet we are free.

If freedom comes at the expense of belonging, or if belonging comes at the expense of freedom, then both are compromised. Freedom and belonging aren't inherently in tension with each other. As one develops, so does the other. Freedom and belonging are experienced along a spectrum; they grow as we individuate.

The belief that others need to agree with, approve of, or understand you inhibits your freedom and hinders individuation.

Belonging

Growing up, I felt a strong attachment to being Jewish that I didn't fully understand. I attempted to find solid intellectual ground for this attachment. But I didn't believe that the Bible contained an accurate account of history, nor did I find all Jewish rituals compelling.

The form of Judaism in which I immersed myself for many years divided life into three spheres: belonging, believing, and behaving. Of these three, belonging was understood to be primary. Beliefs and behaviors were of secondary importance. I maintained this orientation for many years.

An identity built upon beliefs struck me as inherently weak. Beliefs can be challenged, and they tend to change over time. The foundational belief that Jewish teachings are the only true revelation from God was never compelling to me.

Belonging provided a strong base upon which I could build. The Jewish people are a historical reality. Grounding my Jewish identity in belonging was true to my lived experience. And through belonging to the Jewish people, I felt I had a place in the world.

Over time, this sense of belonging was challenged when the Jewish community didn't behave in the ways I wanted. And my belonging was challenged when others were inhospitable toward Jews.

Groups won't always behave according to your wishes. This is true for groups you belong to and groups you don't belong to.

The belief that the rest of the world should behave in ways that meet with your approval inhibits belonging.

People and groups will behave as they behave. If belonging requires that others play their roles in accordance with your imagination, you will find your belonging is always incomplete.

Beliefs

Beliefs are products of our imaginations. Like other products of our imaginations, beliefs are ephemeral and unreliable. They can be fun to play with, but on a certain level, they aren't real.

When enough people share a belief, it can have real-life consequences. The legal entities we call corporations are products of our imaginations. Money is a similar imaginative exercise, as are nations. Corporations, money, and nations have real-life consequences. Yet they are created by our imaginations and agreements, so in this sense, they aren't real.

"Belonging to the Jewish people" is a similar belief. It has real-life consequences, but on a fundamental level it is a fiction. I had thought that basing my Jewish attachments on belonging provided a firmer ground than basing my attachments on beliefs. The discovery that belonging to the Jewish people is a belief came as a surprise.

There is no rule of nature that says that certain humans must be Jews, while others must be Christians, Muslims, atheists, and so on. Similarly, there is no rule of nature that insists that some people must be Canadians while others are Americans, Italians, Chinese, etc.

Belonging to a group is part of our constructed identity. When we imagine ourselves belonging to a specific group or community, we create an "us." And the creation of "us" brings "them" into existence. When we create "them" we create a group we exclude and from which we are excluded.

Dividing the world into "us and them" is a standard human experience. Being part of a group requires the existence of others who aren't part of the group.

We will sometimes go to great lengths to help people we don't know because they are part of "us." And treating others as "them" can cause great harm. Being part of a group can lead to both wonderful and terrible outcomes. Being part of a group is a belief; it is part of our constructed identity.

The belief that others need to agree with, approve of, or understand you inhibits your freedom. To be free, learn to drop this belief and ignore demands that you be anything other than yourself.

The belief that a person, or a group of people, should be anything other than they are inhibits your belonging. To belong, learn to drop this belief and accept that people are exactly as they are.

Investigating Beliefs

As a congregational rabbi, I learned to engage with people's beliefs based on how they functioned for the believer.

There are a few questions I learned to ask about beliefs. Some of these questions are pragmatic. Select a belief that you would like to examine and ask yourself:

- ✦   How is this belief functioning?
- ✦   What behaviors does it lead to?

+ What attitudes does this belief encourage?

It is interesting to note that beliefs often increase, rather than reduce, suffering.

Many beliefs offer a sense of control. Giving up fantasies of control may be uncomfortable. If we learn to distinguish between what we can and cannot change, we'll eliminate a great deal of suffering.

> *God, grant me the serenity to accept the things*
> *I cannot change, the courage to change the things I*
> *can, and the wisdom to know the difference.*
> —Reinhold Niebuhr

Other questions about beliefs are more fundamental:

+ Is this belief true? (Before responding, imagine that your life and the lives of all those you love depend on whether your response is correct.)
+ How do I know that it is true?
+ What would happen if I no longer held this belief?
+ Who would I be without this belief?

It is interesting to see how many beliefs are shaken loose when closely examined.

Belief vs. Experience

Belief in God might be a story we tell ourselves. Belief that there is *no* God is a different story we might tell ourselves.

I have found that focusing on what I believe is much less productive than focusing on my experience.

For example, rather than focus on whether I believe in God, I ask myself the question "Who What Where am I?" or "What is here?"

If I ask the question sincerely, sit quietly, and don't rush to provide a verbal answer, the response emerges from my experience. Whether this experience is labeled God or something else doesn't matter.

A belief in God may be helpful. It may motivate ethical behaviors and lead to an experience of your true nature.

A belief that there is no God may function similarly. Belief in no God may keep the focus on the near-at-hand experience of existing as a human. And this may motivate ethical behaviors and lead to an experience of your true nature.

In a similar manner, both belief in God and belief that there is no God can be misleading. Beliefs may lead you astray or they may point you in a helpful direction. Usually, they do some measure of both.

I can't tell you whether belief in God or belief that there is no God is a "good" belief for you. I can only tell you that both are beliefs, a story you are telling yourself.

Letting go of the belief and opening yourself up to experience will ground you. Instead of insisting that an idea in your head is true, allow experience to be your guide.

For example, I don't believe in the chair I'm sitting in. Instead, I experience the chair by sitting in it. Whether I believe in the chair ceases to be a meaningful question.

Instead of believing or not believing, trust your experience. The vocabulary you develop to communicate about your experience may or may not include the word *God*.

Either way, it doesn't matter. You are no longer trying to convince yourself or someone else about an idea. Instead, you have experienced a certain reality and your experience, not beliefs about your experience, is your truth.

Beliefs and opinions are products of our minds. They exist in our imaginations rather than in reality. But that doesn't stop us from having beliefs and opinions.

Our beliefs and opinions are probably not true. Remember, truth includes all perspectives, from A to Z. But our beliefs and opinions can exert tremendous influence upon us. Unless we are conscious of our mental processes, our minds don't distinguish between what we know from experience and what we believe.

And to make things more difficult, our reflections upon lived experience will sometimes lead us astray.

We have an experience. We could just sit with the experience and allow it to be. Instead, we usually place layers of interpretation upon our experience. Then, we mistake the interpretations for the experience itself.

Our minds and memories are notoriously fallible. It is difficult for us to distinguish between the truth of the lived experience and the memory and interpretation of that experience.

Experience can mislead us in other ways too. For example, we can experience cold, even when the temperature around us is objectively hot. "Cold" was the experience, even though "hot" was the temperature.

The goal isn't to stop having beliefs, opinions, and memories, or to stop interpreting our experiences. Instead, we should recognize their undependable nature. We should learn to hold our beliefs, opinions, memories, and inter-pretations a bit more lightly.

We can still dedicate ourselves to ideas. We can believe that corporations exist, that money has value, and that we are citizens of a nation. And we can believe in the values of liberty, equality, cooperation, and so on. But we will also be aware that beliefs are products of our imaginations. Improving upon our ability to distinguish between reality and imagination leads us to hold our beliefs more lightly.

As children, we had active imaginations. Perhaps with some exceptions, we were able to distinguish between imagination and reality. As adults, we seem to lose some of this ability. We regularly mistake our creative imaginings for reality. We forget that corporations, money, nations, and much else in our lives are the products of our imaginations. We play a grown-up version of make-believe, but we have forgotten how to recognize reality outside of the game.

As children, games could sometimes upset us. When this happened, someone might have reminded us that "it's only a game." When we forget it's a game, it can diminish our enjoyment.

Knowing that we, and others just as talented and smart, have been led astray by ideas should make us humble. Ideas can be fun to play with. And ideas can create real-life conse-quences, for good or for ill. Ideas have a role to play in our lives, but if we live only in the world of ideas, we will miss out on the

> **If we live only in the world of ideas, we will miss out on the creative energy that lies behind them.**

creative energy that lies behind them. This energy lies prior to language and gives rise to language so it cannot be fully captured in words. It is infinitely more powerful than the most powerful idea. This energy grounds our lives in truth.

The alternative is to ground our lives in imagination, interpretation, memory, and opinion.

Our constructed identities provide a great deal of excitement and drama. They also provide unnecessary suffering. If you are content to live from your constructed identity, you will probably continue to do so. But if you are deeply curious about the nature of who you are, or if you are strongly motivated to decrease suffering, you will keep exploring your unconstructed identity. Either way, it is your life to lead and who is to say that one way is better than another? The choice is up to you.

Who Is Free? And Who Belongs?

To fulfill our desires to belong, we look to our family, friends, community, nation, and many other places as well. All can only provide partial satisfaction to our desire to belong. When these places fail to fully satisfy our desire to belong, we tend to put the blame on them. We tell ourselves that if they fixed their flaws, we would finally experience the satisfaction of belonging.

This is a false belief produced by ego.

And when we feel our freedom is constrained, we often blame our circumstances.

This is another false belief produced by ego. Ego works hard to keep us dissatisfied.

While he was in prison in the Soviet Union, Natan Sharansky was subject to interrogations. During these interrogations, he would tell his captors anti-Soviet jokes.

> *And they were almost bursting with laughter and they could not. And I said to them, "You cannot even laugh when you want to laugh, and you want to tell me that I'm in prison and you're free?"*[2]

For years, I was like the captors in this story. I was caught within the drama of my constructed identity. My thoughts tended to repeat themselves. And many of them had an underlying negative message: "The world shouldn't be as it is. It should be the way I want it to be!"

Eventually, I got tired of the drama. I noticed that being lost in my thoughts didn't accomplish anything. And my thoughts were often agitating and annoying. "Oh," I would say to my thoughts with a sense of exasperation, "it's you again."

I'm not suggesting that thoughts have no value. Thinking is an amazing tool that should be used often. And it's worthwhile to make the effort to become better at it.

Conscious awareness can use thinking as a tool. But so can ego. And when ego uses the tool of thinking, it usually makes us miserable. Ego will often use thinking to sow fear and dissatisfaction.

Today, I can still get stuck in repetitive and negative thoughts. But I will typically catch myself and recognize that ego is, once again, working hard to gain control.

Once I catch myself, I remember that the only thing blocking my experience of peace, contentment, freedom, and belonging is my insistence that they don't already exist. Instead of grasping for these experiences, I am able to recognize that they are already present.

Our families, friends, community, nation, etc., are imperfect. And our circumstances include at least some restrictions on our ability to do what we want, when we want. But despite these imperfections and restrictions, freedom and belonging are still available to us.

How can freedom and belonging become the truth of our lived experience?

To answer this question, we need to return to the root question of WhoWhatWhere is this thing called "I?"

The truth of our existence is that an alert awareness lies beneath and beyond ego. "You" are not aware. Awareness is aware. What we typically call "me" refers to ego. It is a cloak worn by awareness that can be taken off and put back on.

To what does this awareness belong?

This awareness belongs to everything. It is the creative energy that courses through all that exists.

Is this awareness free?

This awareness is pure potential. It is an energy that can be transformed into an endless variety of thoughts and material forms. It contains a boundless freedom.

Group belonging is a game played by ego. Belonging to a group, or not belonging, feeds the process of identity construction. Egoic, separation consciousness plays the game of dividing the world into us and them. Egoic con-sciousness wants to make us good and them bad.

Egoic consciousness is a part of being human. The goal is not to destroy ego. The goal is to allow ego to work for you rather than against you.

Unity consciousness will allow egoic consciousness to play its game of groups. Unity consciousness can appreciate the value and fun of having an us. But unity consciousness will disrupt the impulse to make us good and them bad. Unity consciousness understands that on a deeper level, there are no groups, no us and them. There is only the one that we are.

If these words about freedom and belonging remain in the realm of ideas, they will be unsatisfying. Ideas of freedom and belonging won't create the experience.

But if quiet awareness takes its place as the center from which you live, then you can allow everyone to be exactly as they are. Your desires for freedom and belonging may finally be satisfied.

Personally, I still have a long way to go. But I have had enough of a taste of the freedom and belonging that are our birthright to know that this is more than theory.

This year we are slaves; next year we shall be free.

Embodied Spirit

My background and experiences are part of the totality of who I am. When I identify as a Jew, or as an American, these identities don't prevent living from conscious aware-ness. Constructing identity is part of what it means to be a human being. These identities are incredible creations. The dance of living with both unconstructed and constructed identity is an amazing adventure.

The challenge is to hold constructed identity loosely, inhabit it fully, and live from unconstructed identity.

Over time, the nothing that is everything has penetrated my life more deeply. The individuation process has advanced. I have become better at both "standing apart from" and "standing together with." Freedom and belonging have grown.

> Hold constructed identity loosely, inhabit it fully, and live from unconstructed identity.

Compared to my past, I spend less time trapped within ego, and live more frequently from conscious awareness. More of my life is lived in a state of flow. And more of my actions arise from love. But ego still shows up every day, sometimes for hours on end.

Because living from ego is a regular feature of my life, instead of experiencing belonging, I often feel I'm on the outside looking in. And I regularly sense that freedom is constrained by my perceived limits. Perhaps over time, I will live from ego less and less. If I do, I expect my sense of freedom and belonging will continue to expand.

For many years, I would read words that pointed me in the direction of the insights presented in this book. I thought I understood those words, but I was stuck in ego's understanding.

At best I understood that the essence of my being was connected to an alert awareness. I could often sense this awareness through prayer, meditation, being in nature, and in other experiences.

I thought I was the subject of these experiences. I didn't understand that awareness was having an experience of being consciously aware of itself. "I" was, and is, an illusion created by ego.

There is a saying often quoted in spiritual circles: "We aren't human beings having spiritual experiences. We are spiritual beings having human experiences."

My ego understood "We are spiritual beings having human experiences" to mean that "I" as an individual human entity, was a spiritual being. With this understanding, ego maintained its sovereignty.

A deeper understanding is not that I am a spiritual being or even that we are spiritual beings, but that there is only being. In the realm of being, the concepts of *spiritual* and *non-spiritual* cease to have meaning. In the realm of being, there is no "we" and no "I," at least not as we usually use these words.

When the ego illusion is allowed to rule, it uses everything it can to maintain its sovereignty. Including, and perhaps especially, spiritual and moral teachings.

When the ego illusion is fully recognized, then everything it has so painstakingly constructed falls apart.

Ego constructs the desires for freedom and belonging. Pure being, the nothing that is everything, appears to be perfectly comfortable living as a human who longs for freedom and belonging.

And pure being is also perfectly comfortable living as a human who has recognized that freedom and belonging are our birthright. We can't attain them because we've always had them. We just don't always realize that we have them.

You belong and you are free in much the same way that trees belong and are free. But this understanding is flawed as well. You are free and you belong in the way that humans are free and belong. Or even better, you are free and belong in the special way that your particular life form is free and belongs.

You can stop struggling to belong. And you can stop yearning for freedom.

You belong and you are free.

Key Takeaways

- Freedom means granting everyone, including yourself, the right to be exactly who they are.
- Belonging to a group is a belief.
- Beliefs can have real-life consequences, but they aren't real.
- The process of individuation involves learning to simultaneously "stand apart from" and "stand together with."
- Hold your constructed identity loosely, inhabit it fully, and live from unconstructed identity.
- Ego constructs the desires for freedom and belonging.
- Freedom and belonging are our birthright. We can't attain them because we've always had them.
- When we live from conscious awareness, we experience our freedom and our belonging.

Chapter 8

Death, Healing, and Love

Clasp the world, but with relaxed hands; embrace it,
but with open arms.

—Rabbi Milton Steinberg

DURING YOUR FIRST FEW MONTHS of life, you weren't aware of having a body. You existed, but you didn't locate your existence in your body. You first realized you had a body when you were around four months old.

You soon realized that your body could be hurt. Having a body makes you vulnerable. Eventually, you recognized that your body won't last forever. You are mortal.

In Eden, Adam and Eve were naked and unashamed. This changes when they eat from the forbidden tree.

Then the eyes of both of them were opened and
they knew they were naked; they sewed fig leaves
and made themselves coverings.[1]

Why is nudity their first realization? And why is covering themselves the first thing they do after eating from the tree?

The Adam and Eve story is about entering a different stage of consciousness, one where they are aware of their bodies. Before eating the fruit, they were like newborns. They were unaware of their bodies and so they weren't aware of their mortality. When they become aware of their bodies, they realize they are naked. They also realize that their bodies won't last forever, that they are mortal.

They would prefer to be immortal.

Grasping for an unobtainable physical immortality, the mind attempts to dominate its surroundings. By asserting power over nature, the mind imagines it is making progress toward the immortality it seeks. Sometimes the desire to be immortal motivates noble purposes, such as leaving a meaningful legacy or making advancements in the field of medicine. But attempts to achieve immortality are doomed to failure.

From the perspective of the mind, the body is an ever-present reminder that we will die. The existence of the body mocks the mind's quest for immortality.

Adam and Eve cover themselves because they are ashamed. They aren't ashamed of the physical appearance of their bodies. They are ashamed they *have* bodies.

During my last few years of living in spiritual seeking mode, I began to exercise. I had read that if you don't engage in weight bearing exercise as you age, you will lose muscle mass. Lifting suitcases into airplane overhead bins had already become more difficult. The prospect of becoming ever weaker was unappealing.

I started with Pilates and soon added yoga. I have been practicing yoga for more than a decade.

It is telling that I came to exercise after reading about losing muscle mass. I lived within my thoughts. I needed a thought to lead me to the wisdom of the body.

I was initially drawn to yoga for its physical benefits. I soon learned that my body was not separate from my mind (thoughts) and spirit (the conscious awareness that we are). Physical changes from exercising were accompanied by emotional, intellectual, and spiritual growth. Perhaps I would have left the perpetual loop of spiritual seeking behind even if I hadn't practiced yoga. But I am certain the practice of yoga served as a catalyst.

The word *yoga* means to yoke, join, or unite.

I would like to say that upon leaving spiritual seeking behind, I experienced a complete unification of body, mind, and spirit. But this wouldn't be true. Integration of body, mind, and spirit has been an ongoing process. My yoga practice has helped keep this process alive and moving forward.

In yoga, every body, from the movie star's and the athlete's to the regular Jane and John Doe's, bumps up against its limitations. The body's natural abilities are relatively unimportant in yoga. Everyone starts where they are and seeks to grow from there.

The yoga classes I have attended have been filled with all types of people. Bodies come in all shapes and sizes—short, tall, fat, thin, muscular, lithe, and everything in between. People with all these shapes and sizes practice yoga. Bodies that appear much less fit than my own are frequently capable of doing things that my body struggles to manage. I have been impressed with the abilities of all these body types to take on the challenges presented by yoga. Moreover, I have been impressed with the people inhabiting these bodies as they advance themselves through the practice of yoga.

Yoga has helped me accept my body. My natural physical gifts aren't a particular place of pride. Nor are my physical limitations a source of anxiety or personal diminishment.

Your body's gifts and limitations, and your mind's gifts and limitations, are part of what make you uniquely you. They provide a canvas on which to work—and the work isn't better or worse based on your physique or IQ. Your focus and intention determine the quality of your experience.

Your body is a good body because it is where you live. It gives you a home in this world.

By connecting with the body, we can regain access to the wisdom of an integrated existence and experience life as an organic flow. When the illusory division between mind, body, and spirit is washed away, we are left with a calm, quiet knowing.

Yoga has helped me see the way that spirit shines within the physical form of the body. Yoga's emphasis on strength, flexibility, and balance provides a doorway. Eventually, yoga teaches the wise practitioner to move the body's energy, including mental energy, in life-supporting ways. Yoga is not the only path to these experiences, but for me, it has been a helpful one.

Your body, regardless of its strengths and limitations, whether it is strong or weak, healthy or ill, is your home in this world. It enables the conscious awareness that is you to experience the world in human form.

> A good body is the one you have.

A good body is the one you have.

Healing

Around eighteen hundred years ago, a Jewish sage named Abaye composed a prayer to be recited after going to the bathroom. The prayer is still in use today.

> *Blessed are You, God of the universe, who formed human beings with wisdom, creating people with many openings and many tubes. It is clearly evident that if even one of them would be opened, or if even one of them would be closed, it would be impossible to survive and to stand before You even for one hour. Blessed are You, God, who heals all flesh and acts wondrously.*

To understand the essence of this type of prayer, look at the statements that begin "Blessed are You, God..." This prayer contains two such statements.

The first "Blessed are You" statement expresses appreciation for the design of the human body. The second praises God "who heals all flesh and acts wondrously."

Before going to the bathroom, are you sick? And after relieving yourself, have you been healed? What does going to the bathroom have to do with healing?

When you eat, you take foreign matter into your body. Your body processes this matter and uses what it can to sustain you.

Some of the matter you take in has the potential to cause harm. The liver and kidneys process the potentially harmful materials, which are eliminated from your body when you go to the bathroom. Without the ability to process and eliminate, you would be poisoned and die.

We are engaged in a continuous process of healing.

The healing process isn't only about eliminating physical waste from our bodies. We are constantly processing physical, emotional, intellectual, and spiritual content, even if we are unaware of it. Ideally, we follow the example of the body. We retain nutritious, life-enhancing, content and we eliminate that which may become harmful to us. When healing is understood to mean wisely incorporating and eliminating, then learning is a type of healing, relationships involve healing, and spiritual development is about healing.

People can be exposed to terrible, toxic, circumstances and still find the wherewithal to rise above. These people inspire us. When we witness the depth of the human capacity to emerge from crushing difficulties, we are amazed. On a less grand scale, we enact this capacity every day. We encounter positive and negative content daily. We contend with the negative and hopefully incorporate, and then integrate the positive.

Our ability to take in all types of content—physical, emotional, intellectual, and spiritual—retain value from it, and eliminate what is harmful, is, in the words of the prayer, wondrous.

Healing that takes place on one level can affect the others. For example, I found that the seemingly mundane process of strengthening my upper back and opening my shoulders made it easier for me to access my emotions. Literally and metaphorically, I became more openhearted.

I began exercising for purely physical reasons. Unexpectedly, the practice of yoga has helped me grow in multiple ways. And it has helped me appreciate and celebrate along the way.

This constant process of healing is one of life's tasks. Take whatever life brings you—food, relationships, ideas, states of consciousness, etc.—then cleanse, eliminate, incorporate, and integrate.

Many religious teachings tell people that if they believe and behave properly, they will have a comfortable place in an afterlife. I was never convinced by these teachings. But part of my attraction to the idea of belonging to the Jewish people was that it conferred a sense of immortality.

I would eventually die, but the Jewish people would live on. By attaching myself to the Jewish people, I had roots in the past and a place in the future.

I was using my understanding of spirituality as being "connected to something beyond myself" to placate ego's desire to live forever. It's true that the Jewish people existed in the past. And they may continue to exist for some time into the future. But nothing is forever.

Endings are with us constantly.

When we speak, we give life to the words we utter. As soon as those words have left our mouths, they disappear into nothingness. Their sounds are no longer heard.

Every inhale comes to an end and yields to an exhale. The exhale ends too and gives way to a new inhale. Each breath is unique, never to be repeated again.

Every word, every step, every breath, ends almost immediately after it is brought to life.

We typically become accustomed to this daily cycle of beginnings and endings. But there are other endings so large they are hard to comprehend.

In about five billion years, the sun is expected to stop shining. Earth as we know it will come to an end.

Our universe is four and a half billion years old. *Homo sapiens* have been around for three hundred thousand years. Civilizations, with characteristics such as culture and writing, began about ten thousand years ago. The universe survived for a long time without us.

Someday, and perhaps within just a few generations, *Homo sapiens* will become extinct. Perhaps the ability to control evolution through gene editing will create a new species. Perhaps we will endure another fate. But at some point, and maybe soon, the time of *Homo sapiens* will come to an end.

The religions and nations we see today may be around for a while, but just like *Homo sapiens* and the sun, they won't exist forever. And they may not exist for very much longer. Our bodies will end. Our communities will end. Our religions will end. Our nations will end. Even our planet won't last forever.

The attempt to deny the truth of death comes from ego. Ego might assert that immortality can be found in the survival of our family, nation, religion, or particular ideas to which we are devoted. On its surface, this appears to be a way to escape ego's grip. But it is still ego imagining its own survival.

For years, I chased immortality by devoting myself to making the world a better place. This altruistic ego disguise is benign and socially constructive. The fact that others received benefit was gratifying. But truth be told, ego was at the root of my motivations. I wanted to make the world a better place because it provided *me* with meaning and purpose. And it held out the promise of a personal legacy that could last into the future.

Today, I still hope that my presence on this planet is socially constructive. But I am no longer tied to fantasies of immortality. And my sense of meaning and purpose isn't measured by how much I've been able to do for others.

One ego might attempt to achieve immortality by freezing its brain. Another might chase immortality by pursuing justice. Given the choice, I'll take the ego devoted to justice every time. But the attempt to achieve immortality is still ego.

This doesn't mean that people, families, ideas, nations, and religions aren't worthwhile. It means that to the extent we value and care for them to satisfy ego's desires for immortality, we are deluding ourselves.

This delusion may have functional value. It can motivate positive behaviors and provide a sense of meaning and purpose. But if service to a larger cause is predicated upon its ability to grant immortality, then the service is based on a false foundation. This type of service is a form of ego-service. And it will fail to attain the desired goal.

In the last chapter, we examined the phrase "we are spiritual beings having a human experience." A common error, and one that I continue to make, is to use this thought to disconnect from the body.

If the focus is primarily on understanding ourselves as "spiritual beings," then it is easy to leave our bodies behind. We need an equal focus on "having a human experience."

> *In order to arrive at spiritual attainment two*
> *gulfs must be crossed: the sea of attachment and the*
> *ocean of detachment.* —Inayat Khan

Having a human experience means living in a body that won't last forever. The story of "your life" will end with "your death." This is the way of things.

The constant stream of endings that accompanies us throughout our lives creates a background awareness of the cycle of death and rebirth. Knowing that every moment and every person will pass away imbues them with a precious sweetness. Mortality creates conditions conducive to love.

> Mortality creates conditions conducive to love.

When we live from ego, we chase immortality. When we live from the nothing that is everything, we become open to service that is rooted in a naturally arising love. This type of love has no end goal and no requirements.

When we are in the presence of a person who has tamed ego and lives from the life force of the universe that is at our center, we can feel something inside relax. We experience the freedom to be ourselves and an appreciation for our uniqueness and beauty. We have the assurance that we will be accepted, even with all our flaws and shortcomings. This sort of love is redemptive. It helps us come home to ourselves.

Although this type of love has no purpose or goal, it is powerful. For those lucky enough to experience it, it can be transformative.

This is not the love of Hollywood movies. This type of love is impersonal and indiscriminate. Loving service of this nature is not about treating a particular person in a special way. It is a general way of being in the world. It shows up in casual exchanges with strangers and in intimate interactions with close friends and family. When our lives are grounded in the pure being that we are, this love arises naturally and spontaneously. It seeks nothing in return and has no purpose beyond itself.

When you recognize ego's tricks, you can live from the pure being that is who you are. Then, at least on occasion, you can bring a redemptive love to yourself and to those you encounter.

Embodying Awareness

The paths of inquiry, listening, and the body that were shared in chapter four are ways to discover the truth of who you are. For a long time, I found I could access this truth when I was alone. When I interacted with others, ego would almost always assume control.

It has taken me some time to learn how to quiet the voice of ego when interacting with others. A helpful practice for me has been to bring attention to the energy of my hands and feet while simultaneously interacting with others. You might choose to try this practice yourself.

Intellectually, I thought this practice might deny others my full attention. But I quickly saw that the practice quieted my mind. Using this technique, I found that rather than being distracted, I was bringing a different quality of presence.

Connecting to the energy and wisdom of the body enhanced my interactions. Eventually, this connection became more natural. It stopped requiring special focus and attention.

I often have thoughts running through my mind as I interact with others. But I have learned that my thoughts don't need to be believed. Some thoughts are helpful. Others are not. I'm still learning to discern which thoughts are, and aren't, worthy of my attention.

The mind and the body are part of who we are, but they aren't the totality of who we are. The mind and the body can serve ego. And the mind and the body can serve conscious awareness.

"I have a body."

According to this sentence, the body is something "I" have, not something that "I" am.

"I have a mind."

The same is true for this sentence. It presupposes that there is an "I" that has a mind.

In reality, neither our mind nor our body is who we truly are. They are a part of us. But they don't define us.

We are awareness.

We are not aware. *Awareness* is aware.

We are consciousness.

We are not conscious. *Consciousness* is conscious.

Who What Where is this "I" that has a mind and body?

Everything that exists, including our best and worst impulses, arises from the same place as everything else that exists. Our bodies, minds, and even time itself are not exceptions to this reality.

An ancient Jewish teaching has an interesting and creative way of capturing this idea. In a system containing 613 commandments, Jewish thought attempts to supply the details for living well. There are 248 positive commandments ("Do this!") and 365 negative commandments ("Don't do that!"). The commandments cover individual and interpersonal behavior, business, agriculture, food, and more.

Within this system, 248 is the number of bones in the human body, and 365 is the number of tendons—and the number of days in a year.

Modern biology counts 206 bones and around 4,000

tendons in the human body. The inaccuracy of the teaching is unimportant. The statement that there are 365 days in a year may also be inaccurate. It depends upon the calendar being used and the particular year (for example, there are 366 days in our leap years). To appreciate the substance of what is being communicated, we need to look past these inaccuracies.

The lesson offered is that the details of living well lie within the design of the body and within time itself.

As we saw in chapter four, YHWH, IsWasWillBe, is a word used by the biblical author(s) to express the pure being that is WhoWhatWhere we are. Running from right to left, the four letters that make up the name YHWH, yod, hey, vav, hey look like this: יהוה

When they are stacked on top of one another, they resemble the human form:

Human beings are pure being. We are this word, YHWH, made flesh.

Loving Service

Within our bodies there are many organs. One of these organs is the liver. Within the liver there are many cells.

Liver cells die all the time, but the liver lives on. The death of an individual liver cell might be a major event in the life of that cell, but the liver is not diminished by the death of one of its cells.

Imagine a liver cell wishing for immortality. One day it thinks it has achieved its dream and refuses to die.

This is called cancer.

The cancerous liver cell will also die. It does not achieve immortality by resisting death. It creates damage.

A healthy liver cell is in service to something greater, the functioning of the liver. To keep the liver healthy, liver cells die. And the liver is in service to something greater as well, the functioning of the body.

Is the body the end point? Or is the body in service to something greater too?

If, as we have said, your identity doesn't lie in your mind or your body, then yes, the body is in service to something greater.

I don't know whether this chain of service ever ends. Ego, on the other hand, is certain that ego itself is the pinnacle of existence.

When life is in service to ego, it becomes devoted to chasing ego's notions of immortality. When life is a conscious expression of the life force of the universe, it becomes devoted to love.

I often wish life weren't filled with death and endings. But my wishing doesn't make it so. And death doesn't negate the value of life.

As the rabbi of a congregation, I interacted with many people encountering illness and death. This constant exposure brought home the reality of mortality. Death can be approached with fear and dread or with equanimity and peace. Regardless of how it is approached, death is a normal and inescapable experience.

With repeated exposure, my fear of death diminished, though it didn't disappear entirely. Entering the unknown still contains some fear. But it also contains possibility. And I try not to be ruled by my fears.

> *I've been absolutely terrified every second of my life. And I've never let it keep me from doing a single thing I wanted to do.* —Georgia O'Keeffe[2]

As the inevitability of death became more clearly apparent, a renewed energy for engaging with life emerged. There will be many eons when we won't be alive on earth. The few years we are here, we can make the most of this adventure. For me, making the most of it includes discovering WhoWhatWhere I am. And it includes integrating that discovery into the mundane experiences of everyday life.

Advanced spirituality isn't about providing an escape. It's about living fully.

If we accept that everything ends, there may be sadness and disappointment as illusions of immortality drop away. But as we let go of this illusion, we may find that life becomes even more precious and sweet. The grandiosity of ego, thinking that it will live forever, gives way to something even grander.

Accepting the reality of death can open us up to a different perception of life. You are part of the unfolding of life itself. You can't fully understand your role in this unfolding. But you can know that life has brought you into being and that whatever role you are playing is yours alone to play.

I don't know what awaits us after we die. But I am certain that the life force operating in the universe will continue to exist long after my body has merged with the earth. And I am an expression of this life force.

If your identity doesn't lie in your thoughts or your body, then perhaps the death of the body is not the end of you.

Before you were born, you lived underwater and didn't breathe. This sounds impossible, but it's true.

What awaits us after we die? I don't know. But I am open to discovery.

KEY TAKEAWAYS

+ Body, mind, and spirit are an integrated whole. Experiencing divisions between these different aspects of ourselves is a call for healing.
+ Healing is the process of taking physical, emotional, intellectual, and spiritual content and wisely cleansing, eliminating, incorporating, and integrating.
+ Mortality creates conditions conducive to love.
+ To the extent that we can live from the pure being that is who we are, we will offer a special kind of love to ourselves and to those whom we encounter.

Conclusion

Carrying Your Own Light

A young rabbi complained to the rabbi of the town of Rizhyn: "When I study, I feel life and light. But the moment I stop, it is all gone. What shall I do?"

The rabbi of Rizhyn replied: "That is like when a person walks through the woods on a dark night, and for a time another joins in, lantern in hand. And then, at a crossroads, they part, and the first person must continue on, stumbling through the darkness.

"If you carry your own light, you need not be afraid of any darkness."

IF YOU ARE CONFUSED ABOUT what you are, this confusion will permeate the rest of your life. The first part of this book was about clearing up this confusion.

Our constructed identities are creative masterpieces. We have exerted great effort developing them, and many aspects of these identities are beautiful. Our constructed identities are necessary for our survival. They should be thoroughly enjoyed and appreciated.

But we are so focused on the creations (our constructed identities) that we may neglect to learn much about the creator. Our unconstructed identities are the artists creating these fabulous identities. WhoWhatWhere is this artist?

The first part of this book brought attention to the artist. WhoWhatWhere are you? You are pure being, conscious awareness, YHWH, quiet stillness…

The abundance of words is due to their inadequacy. That which lies behind your constructed identity can't be captured in words. But it can be experienced.

Finding the answer to WhoWhatWhere you are is not an end point. It marks a new beginning for exploration. Having discovered this new realm, you can begin to investigate. What is here?

Alternatively, you can discover the new realm, turn around, and go back to what is familiar. But don't be surprised if the new realm beckons every now and then, encouraging you to explore it further.

The second part of this book was designed to assist your explorations. Discovering your unconstructed identity brings much into focus:

- It is the nature of constructed identity to resist what is. Living from unconstructed identity, which doesn't attempt to push away or hold on, will lead to greater happiness and joy.

- Unconstructed identity is the gateway to unity consciousness. This consciousness gives rise to its own ethics. From within unity consciousness, loving behaviors arise naturally and spontaneously.

+ Religions and schools of thought have much to offer, but they also have potential pitfalls. Knowing what they can offer and how they can lead you astray may help you along the way.

+ Your desires for freedom and belonging can only be partially satisfied by constructed identity. Your unconstructed identity can lead you to experience full freedom and belonging.

+ Everything ends. Constructed identity imagines that mortality is a problem to be solved.

+ Unconstructed identity gives rise to an indiscriminate, loving presence.

+ Always watch out for ego reasserting itself. Ego is a master of disguise.

Sincere exploration can increase the degree of intimacy with your unconstructed identity. The paths of inquiry, listening, and the body are three possible approaches. And there are others. Find paths that work for you. If you find teachers who can help you along the way, wonderful! But never abdicate your authority. A true teacher will help you achieve independence.

If you choose to explore your unconstructed identity, remember to have fun with it. Enjoy the journey! Your life doesn't need to become a perfect expression of the insights and teachings within this book. Mine certainly isn't. But I am confident that over time you and I can both become better embodiments of these insights. As you develop greater intimacy with the pure being that you are, the rest will arise naturally. This has been my experience.

Acknowledgments

Many people contributed to making this book possible.

The Bnai Keshet community of 1988–2002 taught me that spiritual leadership is much more about the heart than the mind. It took me some time to learn this lesson and I thank them for their patience.

The communities of the Reconstructionist Rabbinical College, 1984–1989 and 2002–2013, contributed to my intellectual and spiritual growth. We challenged each other, grew together, made mistakes, and persevered.

I have never met Adyashanti but he helped me navigate many confusing moments. I offer great thanks to him and to Open Gate Sangha, for making his teachings widely available.

My editor, Ed Levy, forced me to confront problems that I would have preferred to ignore. Writing isn't a solitary endeavor and Ed was my chief collaborator. My copy editor, Jennie Cohen, helped polish the manuscript and make it suitable for print. I consider myself very lucky to have found such wise and talented editors.

Jane Gerhard, Denise Portner, Scott Marmorstein, and Michelle Synnestvedt read an earlier version of this book and provided insightful critiques. I did my best to incorporate their feedback. The shortcomings are all mine.

As my primary yoga teacher, Michelle Synnestvedt has been a physical and spiritual guide as well as a literary one. And I have been blessed to learn from many other yoga teachers as well. Justicia DeClue, Amy Henderson, Zhenja La Rosa, and Naime Jezzeny have all helped me along the way. All these teachers, and especially Michelle, have helped me grow and transform.

To all those from whom I've learned, to their students, and to the students of their students, I wish peace and wholeness, grace and kindness, compassion and love.

My most important thanks go to my family. My sister and brother, Ruth and Jonathan, are always willing to lend an ear and share thoughts and insights. Their companionship is a blessing.

I feel very lucky to say that my parents, Cynthia and Ezra, raised me with love and care. I know not everyone has such good fortune. Their love is with me constantly.

Joe and Eliav, to whom this book is dedicated, raised me as I was raising them. They still raise me up every day.

Kay has been my partner on this journey of life. She has kept me grounded and growing, smiling and laughing. Kay is my favorite critic, greatest booster, and best friend. My life has been shaped by our togetherness and our love. This book would not have been possible without her.

ENDNOTES

CHAPTER 1

1   *Who Am I: The Teachings of Bhagvan Sri Ramana Maharshi*, Sri Ramanasramam, 2010, p. 19

2   Genesis, 2:25

CHAPTER 2

1   Many forms of Buddhism don't include God. Confucianism and Taoism are both atheistic. And many individuals actively identifying with a traditional religion don't believe in God. Spirituality and belief in God are not dependent upon one another. You can believe in God and avoid spirituality. And you can delve into spirituality with, or without, a belief in God.

2   I use the term *ego* differently than Freud. Freud identified ego as the mediator between the instinctual desires of the id and the conscious morality of the superego. I also use this term differently from those who view ego as the enemy of spiritual attainment, or as a synonym for selfishness.

3   Jim Whiting, *Yo-Yo Ma: A Biography*, Greenwood, 2008, p. 58

4   The Hebrew word translated as the name Eve, *Chava*, means life. "Adam and Eve" means "Human and Life."

5   *Bereshit Rabbah*, 9:7. *Bereshit Rabbah* includes commentaries from many people. It was codified (the text was fixed and closed) around 300–500 CE. CE stands for "Common Era" and is also known as AD.

6   Rabbi Menaham Mendl of Kotzk, 1787-1859

7   Genesis 3:9–10

8   Sam Keen, *A Conversation with Ernest Becker*, Psychology Today, 1974, pp. 71-80

9   Ernest Becker deathbed interview with Sam Keen. [https://www.youtube.com/watch?v=RtmD9og-3ZTQ]

CHAPTER 3

1   Maimonides is Moses ben Maimon, 1138–1204. Maimonides is considered one of Judaism's greatest philosophers. Aquinas is Thomas Aquinas, 1225–1274. Aquinas is considered one of Catholicism's greatest philosophers.

2   David Foster Wallace, "This is Water." This talk can be found on YouTube.

3   Thanks to Ezra Klein for articulating this confusion between tired and stressed.

CHAPTER 4

1 Exodus 33:18

2 Exodus 33:19

3 Exodus 33:20–23

4 God's name, YHWH, will be discussed later in this chapter.

5 Exodus 34:5–6

6 Because pronouns referring to God are capitalized in English, translators of the Bible are forced to decide which pronouns refer to God. For this reason, the original text contains greater ambiguity than the English translations.

7 Some people believe that God was the author of the Bible. Others may believe that God dictated the first five books to Moses. Biblical scholars have concluded that the Bible has multiple authors. Scholars believe that the works of these multiple authors were woven together to create a single narrative. This work of weaving could have been the product of a single person, a group of people, or the result of generations of oral tradition. For the purposes of this book, it doesn't matter whether you believe the Bible had a single author or multiple authors. My use of "author(s)" allows the reader to choose their preferred belief.

8 I was first introduced to this translation by Arthur Green in his book *Seek My Face, Speak My Name*, Jason Aronson, 1992.

9 Exodus 33:20

10   Exodus 34:30–31

11   Inayat Khan (1882–1927) was a Sufi teacher.

12   Rumi (1207–1223) was a Sufi poet.

13   Deuteronomy 6:4

14   Papaji (1910–1997) was a disciple of the Hindu sage Ramana Maharshi.

15   Yahya ibn Mu'adh al-Razi (830–871) was a Sufi teacher.

16   *Tao Te Ching: An Insightful and Modern Translation*, J.H. McDonald, QigongVacations.org; 2014, chapter 1. The *Tao Te Ching* is an ancient Chinese work that is the foundational text of Taoism.

17   Copernicus was the sixteenth-century scientist who taught us that the earth isn't the center of the solar system. He discovered that the earth revolved around the sun. The phrase "Copernican revolution" describes a fundamental paradigm shift.

CHAPTER 5

1   I first encountered this articulation in Daniel Matt's article "Beyond the Personal God" from the spring 1994 issue of *The Reconstructionist*. Although I don't quote his article directly, my discussion of the words used to describe a tree is closely indebted to Matt's article.

2   The word *emet*, "truth," is closely related to the widely known Hebrew word *amen*. In the eighteenth century, amen might have been translated as "Yea, verily!" In the twenty-first century, *amen* could well be translated as "true that!"

3   "If you let go a little, you will have a little happiness. If you let go a lot, you will have a lot of happiness. If you let go completely, you will be free." Ajhan Chah. Ajhan Chah (1918–1992) was a Thai Buddhist monk.

4   Talmud, Brachot 10a. Bruriah and Meir lived in the second century, CE. The Talmud is a multi-volume work that was composed over hundreds of years. It was codified around 400 CE.

5   Talmud, Pesachim 50b

6   My reading here is inspired by a commentary on this verse by Rabbi Menahem Mendel Schneerson in *Derekh Mitzvotekha*. I was introduced to this commentary by Arthur Green. "Now this inclusion really takes place only when a person demonstrates with his very self and body that he loves his neighbor, like two limbs joined to one another, fulfilling 'What's mine is yours,' for the other is his own flesh and blood." Arthur Green, *Devotion and Commandment*, HUC Press, 1989, p. 68

7   Inayat Khan, from a talk given to his students.

Chapter 6

1   Franz Rosenzweig, *On Jewish Learning*, Schocken, 1955

2   I first heard this analogy to holding a ball from Adyashanti. Adyashanti (born 1962) is an American spiritual teacher.

3   The translated blessing is "Blessed are You, God, ruler of the universe, who remembers the covenant, is faithful to the covenant, and keeps the promise."

CHAPTER 7

1   Talmud, Bava Batra 11a
2   https://www.timesofisrael.com/at-toi-event-sharansky-talks-of-freedom-and-how-israel-went-wrong-propping-up-a-dictator

CHAPTER 8

1   Genesis 3:7
2   Georgia O'Keeffe (1887–1986) was an American artist.

I HOPE YOU ENJOYED READING *Where Are You?: A Beginner's Guide to Advanced Spirituality*. If you would like to contact me, you can message me through my web site, www.danehrenkrantz.com. And please consider subscribing to my free newsletter, *Not So Random Thoughts*, which can be found at danehrenkrantz.substack.com or by scanning the QR code below.

I look forward to hearing from you.

Printed in Great Britain
by Amazon

11872251R00109